W9-BYR-896

Living in Renaissance Italy

Living in Renaissance Italy

Titles in the Series Include:

Living in Renaissance Italy

Mark R. Nesbitt, *Book Editor*

Bruce Glassman, *Vice President*
Bonnie Szumski, *Publisher*
Helen Cothran, *Managing Editor*

GREENHAVEN PRESS
An imprint of Thomson Gale, a part of The Thomson Corporation

THOMSON
━━━━━✦━━━━━™
GALE

Detroit • New York • San Francisco • San Diego • New Haven, Conn.
Waterville, Maine • London • Munich

Gloucester Library
P.O. Box 2380
Gloucester, VA 23061

945.05 LIV 79 7/07

© 2005 Thomson Gale, a part of The Thomson Corporation.

Thomson and Star Logo are trademarks and Gale and Greenhaven Press are registered trademarks used herein under license.

For more information, contact
Greenhaven Press
27500 Drake Rd.
Farmington Hills, MI 48331-3535
Or you can visit our Internet site at http://www.gale.com

ALL RIGHTS RESERVED.
No part of this work covered by the copyright hereon may be reproduced or used in any form or by any means—graphic, electronic, or mechanical, including photocopying, recording, taping, Web distribution or information storage retrieval systems—without the written permission of the publisher.

Every effort has been made to trace the owners of copyrighted material.

Cover credit: © Alinari/Art Resource, NY. *Fish Market*, by Joachim Beuckelaer.
Corel, 107
National Library of Medicine, 59
Planet Art, 17, 25, 99

LIBRARY OF CONGRESS CATALOGING-IN-PUBLICATION DATA

Living in Renaissance Italy / Mark R. Nesbitt, book editor.
   p. cm. — (Exploring cultural history)
  Includes bibliographical references and index.
  ISBN 0-7377-2809-4 (lib. : alk. paper)
    1. Renaissance—Italy. 2. Italy—Civilization—1268–1559. 3. Italy—Social life and customs. I. Nesbitt, Mark R., 1970– . II. Series.
  DG445.L58 2005
  945'.05—dc22
                                      2004059674

Printed in the United States of America

Contents

Chapter 4: Religion and Honor

Foreword

Too often, history books and teachers place an overemphasis on events and dates. Students learn that key births, battles, revolutions, coronations, and assassinations occurred in certain years. But when many centuries separate these happenings from the modern world, they can seem distant, disconnected, even irrelevant.

The reality is that today's society is *not* disconnected from the societies that preceded it. In fact, modern culture is a sort of melting pot of various aspects of life in past cultures. Over the course of centuries and millennia, one culture passed on some of its traditions, in the form of customs, habits, ideas, and beliefs, to another, which modified and built on them to fit its own needs. That culture then passed on its own version of the traditions to later cultures, including today's. Pieces of everyday life in past cultures survive in our own lives, therefore. And it is often these morsels of tradition, these survivals of tried and true past experience, that people most cherish, take comfort in, and look to for guidance. As the great English scholar and archaeologist Sir Leonard Woolley put it, "We cannot divorce ourselves from our past. We are always conscious of precedents . . . and we let experience shape our views and actions."

Thus, for example, Americans and the inhabitants of a number of other modern nations can pride themselves on living by the rule of law, educating their children in formal schools, expressing themselves in literature and art, and following the moral precepts of various religions and philosophies. Yet modern society did not invent the laws, schools, literature, art, religions, and philosophies that pervade it; rather, it inherited these things from previous cultures. "Time, the great destroyer, is also the great preserver," the late, noted thinker Herbert J. Muller once observed. "It has preserved . . . the immense accumulation of products, skills, styles, customs, institutions, and ideas that make the man on the American street indebted to all the peoples of history, including some who never saw a street." In this way, ancient Mesopotamia gave the world its first cities and literature; ancient Egypt, large-scale architecture; ancient Israel, the formative concepts of Judaism,

Christianity, and Islam; ancient Greece, democracy, the theater, Olympic sports, and magnificent ceramics; ancient China, gunpowder and exotic fabrics; ancient Rome and medieval England, their pioneering legal systems; Renaissance Italy, great painting and sculpture; Elizabethan England, the birth of modern drama; and colonial America, the formative environments of the founders of the United States, the most powerful and prosperous nation in world history. Only by looking back on those peoples and how they lived can modern society understand its roots.

Not all the products of cultural history have been so constructive, however. Most ancient Greeks severely restricted the civil rights and daily lives of women, for instance; the Romans kept and abused large numbers of slaves, as did many Americans in the years preceding the Civil War; and Nazi Germany and the Soviet Union curbed or suppressed freedom of speech, assembly, and religion. Examining these negative aspects of life in various past cultures helps to expose the origins of many of the social problems that exist today; it also reminds us of the ever-present potential for people to make mistakes and pursue misguided or destructive social and economic policies.

The books in the Greenhaven Press Exploring Cultural History series provide readers with the major highlights of life in human cultures from ancient times to the present. The family, home life, food and drink, women's duties and rights, childhood and education, arts and leisure, literacy and literature, roads and means of communications, slavery, religious beliefs, and more are examined in essays grouped by theme. The essays in each volume have been chosen for their readability and edited to manageable lengths. Many are primary sources. These original voices from a past culture echo through the corridors of time and give the volume a strong feeling of immediacy and authenticity. The other essays are by historians and other modern scholars who specialize in the culture in question. An annotated table of contents, chronology, and extensive bibliography broken down by theme add clarity and context. Thus, each volume in the Greenhaven Press Exploring Cultural History series opens a unique window through which readers can gaze into a distant time and place and eavesdrop on life in a long vanished culture.

Introduction: Life During the Renaissance—Adapting to Many Changes

The Italian Renaissance refers to the rebirth of classic study and explosion of art and culture that took place in the fifteenth and sixteenth centuries. Often seen as the transition period between the medieval period and the modern age, the Renaissance bore the marks of both.

The Renaissance can accurately be described as the last great push of medieval man, carrying on the traditions of towering architecture, high church, and nobility. It can be seen equally as well as the beginning of modern man, when new ideals of individualism, expression, and upward social mobility took hold. Thus, men and women of the Renaissance worked through a time of intense change by holding fast to some of the foundation of the old world while releasing other facets and embracing innovative new ways of thinking and living.

One of the most important areas of change during the Renaissance was in the realm of economics and politics. According to many historians, these changes provided the conditions for the rebirth and explosion of art and culture to take hold. Although renewals of ancient teachings and pockets of artistic and architectural development had occurred throughout the Middle Ages, most simply flared up and died down quickly. These movements took root and flourished during the Renaissance largely because of a terrible tragedy.

Economic Changes

The Black Plague, which hit Europe between 1347 and 1351, killed between one-third and one-half of the population. This dramatic loss of life had a huge impact on the economy of the day.

During the Middle Ages, wealth and power rested in the hands of the nobility, who owned most of the land and thus controlled the agrarian economy. The food and raw materials produced on these lands—including fruits, vegetables, grains, meat, wood, and wool—formed the basis of the entire economy. A small middle class of craftsmen and merchants also existed, though their livelihood depended on selling products exclusively to wealthy noblemen. The gulf that existed between these two classes was vast, and no mechanism for upward mobility existed. Most of the population fell into the lower class, the common laborers and serfs who worked the farmland owned by the nobility. These men and women worked for subsistence wages, which they used to pay the landowner for rent, farming equipment, and protection.

When the plague struck, this system changed dramatically. With a natural disaster like the plague, the accumulated wealth of those who died was passed along to their surviving family members. The dramatic reduction in the number of people who shared the family fortune allowed the surviving members to become much better off financially.

The effect of this was felt in all sectors of society. Lesser nobles found that they now had the resources to rival their neighbors and competitors. Those in the middle class often accumulated enough wealth to move toward the upper classes or at least to solidify their positions and move up within their own class. In addition, the plague largely put an end to the practice of serfdom. Because the plague killed so many peasants, those who were left could choose to work for whomever they wanted, or the people who would pay them the most. This led to a further redistribution of wealth, as the peasants were able to earn more than a subsistence wage. Meanwhile, the increasing labor costs reduced the nobility's position as the ruling class.

With the vast decrease in population that the plague brought, the amount of available housing, farmland, and food increased. The increase in supply led to a decrease in price. Workers could now work less while earning more money. This increase in disposable income affected not just the former serf but the merchant as well. As the economy switched from a largely agrarian one, the power of the nobility, with its vast landholdings, continued to decrease in favor of the merchant, who sold goods that more people could buy. This left more disposable income for the middle class as well.

Renaissance Italy

The new economy of the early Renaissance produced a large number of people with the ability to spend money on nonessential items. A second change would provide them with a reason to spend that money on art and architecture.

Political Change

The same noble families who controlled the land and economy ruled the political arena of the Middle Ages. These families ruled regions ranging in size from a single town and surrounding farmland to great monarchical empires that stretched across Europe. Through war, treaty, and economic pressure, towns, cities, and regions came to be controlled by several layers of rulers. Monarchs governed large areas, often with many different nobles in charge of various areas under them. These great empires covered all of Europe as the age of the Renaissance approached.

When the plague weakened the economic stature of these ruling families, it also weakened their ability to govern large areas. Lacking financial resources as well as soldiers to wage war and police holdings, the area that could be adequately controlled began to shrink. In addition to the influence of the plague, years of wars, bad political alliances, and infighting had significantly weakened these empires as well. Italy was an early beneficiary of this lessening of control. As the empires of Europe began to shrink, consolidating their armies and resources nearer the capitals, the regions of Italy began to feel less and less of their influence. These areas began to develop their own governments. As the threat of invasion became unlikely, these regions began to think of themselves as independent states. Cities such as Florence and Venice created political structures for self-rule. Areas such as southern Italy and the island of Sicily banded together. Treaties and trade were established between regions. The relative peace of the time allowed for money that would have gone to arms and armies to be used to build these cities.

A new form of government called city-states came into being. Though these states broke from the monarchical model of governance, they often retained some of its characteristics; the most powerful family in the region assumed control and kept it as long as its fortunes held. Some city-states were closer to democracies, with elected officials and rulers (though these elections were held solely by the upper class and the nobles).

The city-state led to an increase in the importance of the city as a center of power and commerce. As the economic changes of the era had taken the focus off farmland and placed it on the production of goods and trade, so the political changes refocused the attention of the rich and powerful from controlling huge areas of land to developing and securing the cities.

As these city-states developed, so did competition between them. This competition took the form of competing in beauty and sophistication. City-states began to build great palaces, churches, and public spaces. They paid artists, architects, and sculptors to outdo their neighboring cities. For example, paintings and sculpture were ordered to attest to the grandeur of the city. Michelangelo's statue of David, commissioned by Florence, symbolized the great power and status of the relatively small city by alluding to the triumph of David over Goliath. Mythological as well as religious symbols were used. Baccio Bandinelli created a huge statue of Hercules, considered the protector of Florence, that stood in the Piazza Signoria, the main public square of the city. Venice showed its incredible flair for architecture with the majestic Piazza San Marco, or St. Mark's Square. This large public space faces the main canal of Venice and showcases several of its beautiful buildings. Venice was also known for its great painters. In the Palazzo Ducale, the palace of the duke, the walls and ceilings are adorned with scenes depicting the glory of Venice painted by Tintoretto, Veronese, and other great masters. Many of the Florentine painters were commissioned by Rome to paint the great cathedrals. Michelangelo painted the ceiling of the Sistine Chapel, depicting the story of the book of Genesis. This spectacular ceiling is often considered one of the greatest achievements of the Renaissance.

According to George Holmes, professor of history at Oxford University, "The city [was] important for its accumulation of wealth, spread among a number of free citizens rather than centralized, and for its cultivation of intense competitive intercourse between highly intelligent individuals."[1] Within the cities and regions themselves, competition was fierce as well. Wealthy families tried to outdo each other with extravagant homes and gardens. The explosion of culture and wealth, as well as the breaking down of former social barriers, made it even more important for families to establish themselves and prove their status. Those that came from older, established nobility sought to keep their place in politics and society. Those who had come into money as a result of the new economy worked hard to prove that they belonged.

This competition drove consumerism, which in turn allowed the new economy and political structure to flourish. The political structure and stability provided a protective harbor and impetus for the development of art. In addition, an incredible mix of artistic talent was available at the time. As historian Paul Johnson notes,

As wealth accumulated, those who possessed it gratified their senses by patronizing literature and the arts. . . . But wealth alone would not have produced the phenomenon we call the Renaissance. Money can command art, but it commands in vain if there are no craftsmen to produce it.[2]

Explosion of Art and Artists

During the Middle Ages, artists were considered craftsmen. That is, they were viewed as part of the skilled laborer class, and the art they produced was seen as almost entirely pragmatic. Paintings illustrated historical and religious events and occurrences to the mostly illiterate masses. A church's sculpture and architecture allowed worshippers to experience awe-inspiring surroundings. A castle's art impressed potential enemies with the owner's wealth and grandeur.

This perception changed dramatically during the Renaissance. Author Margaret Aston claims that the artists were "placed . . . on an equality with poets."[3] While the pragmatic uses of art would continue and, in the case of impressing others, in fact grow, a new outlook on art and artists developed. As Johnson at-

Sandro Botticelli's La Primavera *illustrates mythological symbolism, which was a popular theme in Renaissance art.*

tests to, the effects of the new wealth and focus on luxury items resulted in a rapid expansion of the arts:

> Thousands of workshops of all kinds emerged, specializing in stone, leather, metal, wood, plaster, chemicals and fabrics, producing a growing variety of luxury goods and machinery. It was chiefly the families of those who worked in these shops that produced the painters and carvers, the sculptors and architects, the writers and decorators, the teachers and scholars responsible for the huge expansion of culture that marked the beginnings of the early modern age.[4]

Better pay meant shorter hours for all, and higher demand ensured future work and many great artists benefited. Leonardo da Vinci, for example, was the son of a craftsman. When his great gift for sketching was discovered, he was allowed to study under a renowned art teacher, rather than working long hours in his father's shop. Had he been born a hundred years earlier, this may not have been possible.

Born into a time that was ready to receive them, with the economic ability to support their gifts, the artists of the Renaissance were given an incredible stage on which to ply their considerable talents. And ply them they did. The immense wealth of Renaissance art is still a marvel to this day. The great artists of the era—Michelangelo, Leonardo, Filippo Brunelleschi, Donatello—still stand today with the greatest painters, sculptors, and architects the world has ever known.

All of these factors and more contributed to making the Renaissance such a powerful and pervasive force in Italy and throughout Europe. A scholarly movement found support in the new postplague economic and political situation that produced the means, the demand, and the skilled artists to create a great cultural and societal change.

It was indeed a time that produced some of the greatest works of art, the most fantastic architecture and awe-inspiring sculpture of all time. It was also a time that changed the way men and women thought about themselves and the world around them. Perhaps the best way to sum up the impact of the Renaissance comes from Lisa Jardine, a professor at the University of London: "The world we inhabit today, with its ruthless competitiveness, fierce consumerism, restless desire for ever wider horizons, for travel, discovery and innovation . . . is a world which was made in the Renaissance."[5]

Notes

1. George Holmes, *Renaissance*. New York: St. Martin's, 1996, p. 8.

2. Paul Johnson, *The Renaissance*. New York: Random House, 2000, p. 16.

3. Margaret Aston, *The Panorama of the Renaissance*. New York: Henry N. Abrams, 2000, p. 242.

4. Johnson, *The Renaissance*, p. 16.

5. Lisa Jardine, *Worldly Goods*. New York: Nan A. Talese, 1996, p. 436.

Society and Family

CHAPTER
1

Chapter Preface

Of the many changes that took place during the Renaissance, one of the most significant and far reaching was the change in society. Old notions of a static society in which a person maintained the same class position for his or her entire life fell away, replaced by the idea of a mobile society in which one could advance through work and fortune. Yet even as many of the old constructs were falling away, the concept of family as the center of one's life remained.

The new economic opportunities of the fourteenth century provided upward mobility that had not previously existed, and many individuals and families began to make the transition to different social ranks. As the concept of status from birth began to erode, the show of one's wealth and power became increasingly important. Wealth, either from one's family or from hard work and business savvy, became a standard by which to judge an individual's place in society. Although this "capitalistic economic order," as historian Gene Brucker called it, did not totally supplant the medieval notion of status from birth, it did become a driving force in the culture of the day. It was "characterized by risk, uncertainty, flexibility, and sharp fluctuations. It fosters individualism and contributes to social mobility and dislocation through perpetual redistribution of wealth."

In the midst of this flux, however, a medieval conception of family remained the most important connection of the culture. Even as the individualism of the age began to take hold, the family unit stayed firmly intact. Regardless of rank or status, the extended family played a huge role in the life of the individual. What a person did, who he or she married, and where a person lived were dictated by one's family. Those of higher social standing were relentless in securing a good living for their children. They used their wealth and power to secure positions in business, academics, and the church. In addition, marriage was carefully arranged. The goal was to marry into a family that was at least an equal, if not slightly above one's standing.

Extended families lived in proximity to each other, as the male children built or bought houses as close to the family home as possible. Families of wealth and influence would stake their territory, with each succeeding generation becoming more firmly entrenched. Even when neighborhoods changed and certain areas of a city became less desirable, the family that "ruled" that section would stay, even though they could afford to move to a more affluent area.

This combination of new and old, of an upwardly mobile society and a medieval family unit, produced a society in which families rose and fell together. As fortunes were made and lost, social status was gained and taken away, the family stayed together. With one brilliant businessman or craftsman, a family could be propelled to the upper crust of society. Conversely, if one member of the family brought shame or scandal, or if a business venture proved to be a failure, they could lose it all. The glory of one was glory for all. The failure of one could likewise be the ruin of all.

Society and Custom in Urban Italy

Jacob Burckhardt

The Civilization of the Renaissance in Italy, written by renowned
Swiss historian Jacob Burckhardt in 1860, has become one of the
most widely read texts on the topic. In the following excerpt,
Burckhardt discusses the customs of dress and festival during the
Renaissance.

In a society that placed a high value on individualism, fashion
played a large role in establishing oneself. How one dressed told
much about a person, and people went to great lengths to attempt to stand out. The result was a culture of rich, colorful
clothing and adornments. From jewelry to perfume to makeup,
an Italian during the time of the Renaissance used every means
possible to establish his or her position in society.

Another important aspect of the culture of the day was the
many festivals that took place. Just as individuals attempted to
show their worth through their dress, many cities and towns
used festivals to show how wealthy and important they were.
Each festival was a lavish production of sight, sound, and taste.

The outward appearance of men and women [in Italy] and
the habits of daily life were more perfect, more beautiful and
more polished than among the other nations of Europe. The
dwellings of the upper classes fall rather within the province of
the history of art; but we may note how far the castle and the
city mansion in Italy surpassed in comfort, order and harmony
the dwellings of the northern noble. The style of dress varied so
continually that it is impossible to make any complete comparison with the fashions of other countries, all the more because
since the close of the fifteenth century imitations of the latter
were frequent. The costumes of the time, as given us by the Italian painters, are the most convenient, and the most pleasing to

Jacob Burckhardt, *The Civilization of the Renaissance in Italy*, edited and translated by
S.G.C. Middlemore. New York: Penguin Books, 1990.

the eye which were then to be found in Europe; but we cannot be sure if they represent the prevalent fashion, or if they are faithfully reproduced by the artist. It is nevertheless beyond a doubt that nowhere was so much importance attached to dress as in Italy. The nation was, and is, vain; and even serious men among it looked on a handsome and becoming costume as an element in the perfection of the individual. At Florence, indeed, there was a brief period when dress was a purely personal matter, and every man set the fashion for himself, and till far into the sixteenth century there were exceptional people who still had the courage to do so; and the majority at all events showed themselves capable of varying the fashion according to their individual tastes. It is a symptom of decline when Giovanni della Casa[1] warns his readers not to be singular or to depart from existing fashions. Our own age, which, in men's dress at any rate, treats uniformity as the supreme law, gives up by so doing far more than it is itself aware of. But it saves itself much time, and this, according to our notions of business, outweighs all other disadvantages.

In Venice and Florence at the time of the Renaissance there were rules and regulations prescribing the dress of the men and restraining the luxury of the women. Where the fashions were more free, as in Naples, the moralists confess with regret that no difference can be observed between noble and burgher. They further deplore the rapid changes of fashion, and—if we rightly understand their words—the senseless idolatry of whatever comes from France, though in many cases the fashions which were received back from the French were originally Italian. It does not further concern us how far these frequent changes, and the adoption of French and Spanish ways, contributed to the national passion for external display; but we find in them additional evidence of the rapid movement of life in Italy in the decades before and after the year 1500.

We may note in particular the efforts of the women to alter their appearance by all the means which the toilette could afford. In no country of Europe since the fall of the Roman Empire was so much trouble taken to modify the face, the colour of the skin

1. bishop and poet who wrote a book on manners

and the growth of the hair, as in Italy at this time. All tended to the formation of a conventional type, at the cost of the most striking and transparent deceptions. Leaving out of account cos-

Fashion was a significant aspect of Renaissance culture. Carpaccio's Two Venetian Ladies *depicts two well-dressed Italian women.*

tume in general, which in the fourteenth century was in the highest degree varied in colour and loaded with ornament, and at a later period assumed a character of more harmonious richness, we here limit ourselves more particularly to the toilette in the narrower sense.

No sort of ornament was more in use than false hair, often made of white or yellow silk. The law denounced and forbade it in vain, till some preacher of repentance touched the worldly minds of the wearers. Then was seen, in the middle of the public square, a lofty pyre (*talamo*), on which, besides lutes, dice-boxes, masks, magical charms, song-books and other vanities, lay masses of false hair, which the purging fires soon turned into a heap of ashes. The ideal colour sought for both natural and artificial hair was blond. And as the sun was supposed to have the power of making the hair this colour, many ladies would pass their whole time in the open air on sunshiny days. Dyes and other mixtures were also used freely for the same purpose. Besides all these, we meet with an endless list of beautifying waters, plasters and paints for every single part of the face—even for the teeth and eyelids— of which in our day we can form no conception. The ridicule of the poets, the invectives of the preachers and the experience of the baneful effects of these cosmetics on the skin were powerless to hinder women from giving their faces an unnatural form and colour. It is possible that the frequent and splendid representations of mysteries, at which hundreds of people appeared painted and masked, helped to further this practice in daily life. It is certain that it was widely spread, and that the country women vied in this respect with their sisters in the towns. It was vain to preach that such decorations were the mark of the courtesan; the most honourable matrons, who all the year round never touched paint, used it nevertheless on holidays when they showed themselves in public. But whether we look on this bad habit as a remnant of barbarism, to which the painting of savages is a parallel, or as a consequence of the desire for perfect youthful beauty in feature and in colour as the art and complexity of the toilette would lead us to think—in either case there was no lack of good advice on the part of the men.

The use of perfumes, too, went beyond all reasonable limits. They were applied to everything with which human beings came into contact. At festivals even the mules were treated with scents and ointments. Pietro Aretino[2] thanks Cosimo I[3] for a perfumed roll of money. . . .

Festivals

It is by no arbitrary choice that in discussing the social life of this period we are led to treat of the processions and shows which formed part of the popular festivals. The artistic power of which the Italians of the Renaissance gave proof on such occasions was attained only by means of that free intercourse of all classes which formed the basis of Italian society. In northern Europe the monasteries, the courts and the burghers had their special feasts and shows as in Italy; but in the one case the form and substance of these displays differed according to the class which took part in them, in the other an art and culture common to the whole nation stamped them with both a higher and a more popular character. The decorative architecture, which served to aid in these festivals, deserves a chapter to itself in the history of art, although our imagination can only form a picture of it from the descriptions which have been left to us. We are here more especially concerned with the festival as a higher phase in the life of the people, in which its religious, moral and poetical ideas took visible shape. The Italian festivals in their best form mark the point of transition from real life into the world of art.

The two chief forms of festal display were originally here, as elsewhere in the West, the mystery, or the dramatization of sacred history and legend, and the procession, the motive and character of which was also purely ecclesiastical.

The performances of the mysteries in Italy were from the first more frequent and splendid than elsewhere, and were most favourably affected by the progress of poetry and of the other arts. In the course of time not only did the farce and the secular drama branch off from the mystery, as in other countries of Europe, but the pantomime also, with its accompaniments of singing and dancing, the effect of which depended on the richness and beauty of the spectacle.

2. satirist who wrote many comedies and articles, and was often paid by the wealthy not to write about them or to write about their enemies   3. ruler of Florence from 1537 to 1569

The procession, in the broad, level and well-paved streets of the Italian cities, was soon developed into the *trionfo*, or train of masked figures on foot and in chariots, the ecclesiastical character of which gradually gave way to the secular. The processions at the carnival and at the feast of Corpus Christi[4] were alike in the pomp and brilliancy with which they were conducted, and set the pattern afterwards followed by the royal or princely progresses. Other nations were willing to spend vast sums of money on these shows, but in Italy alone do we find an artistic method of treatment which arranged the processions as a harmonious and significative whole.

What is left of these festivals is but a poor remnant of what once existed. Both religious and secular displays of this kind have abandoned the dramatic element—the costumes—partly from dread of ridicule, and partly because the cultivated classes, who formerly gave their whole energies to these things, have for several reasons lost their interest in them. Even at the carnival, the great procession of masks is out of fashion. What still remains, such as the costumes adopted in imitation of certain religious confraternities, or even the brilliant festival of Santa Rosalia[5] at Palermo, shows clearly how far the higher culture of the country has withdrawn from such interests.

The festivals did not reach their full development till after the decisive victory of the modern spirit in the fifteenth century, unless perhaps Florence was here, as in other things, in advance of the rest of Italy. In Florence, the several quarters of the city were, in early times, organized with a view to such exhibitions, which demanded no small expenditure of artistic effort. Of this kind was the representation of hell, with a scaffold and boats in the Arno[6] on 1 May 1304, when the Ponte alla Carraia[7] broke down under the weight of the spectators. That at a later time Florentines used to travel through Italy as directors of festivals (*festaiuoli*) shows that the art was early perfected at home.

In setting forth the chief points of superiority in the Italian festivals over those of other countries, the first that we shall have to remark is the developed sense of individual characteristics, in

4. feast that commemorates the beginning of the sacrament of the Eucharist   5. celebrates a miracle that took place on Pellegrino Mountain when the saint appeared   6. river that runs through Florence   7. bridge over the Arno

other words, the capacity to invent a given mask, and to act the part with dramatic propriety. Painters and sculptors not merely did their part towards the decoration of the place where the festival was held, but helped in getting up the characters themselves, and prescribed the dress, the paints and the other ornaments to be used. The second fact to be pointed out is the universal familiarity of the people with the poetical basis of the show. The mysteries, indeed, were equally well understood all over Europe, since the biblical story and the legends of the saints were the common property of Christendom; but in all other respects the advantage was on the side of Italy. For the recitations, whether of religious or secular heroes, she possessed a lyrical poetry so rich and harmonious that none could resist its charm. The majority, too, of the spectators—at least in the cities—understood the meaning of mythological figures, and could guess without much difficulty at the allegorical and historical, which were drawn from sources familiar to the mass of Italians.

Use of Allegory in Festivals

This point needs to be more fully discussed. The Middle Ages were essentially the ages of allegory. Theology and philosophy treated their categories as independent beings, and poetry and art had but little to add, in order to give them personality. Here all the countries of the West were on the same level. Their world of ideas was rich enough in types and figures, but when these were put into concrete shape, the costume and attributes were likely to be unintelligible and unsuited to the popular taste. This, even in Italy, was often the case, and not only so during the whole period of the Renaissance, but down to a still later time. To produce the confusion, it was enough if a predicate of the allegorical figures was wrongly translated by an attribute. Even Dante[8] is not wholly free from such errors, and, indeed, he prides himself on the obscurity of his allegories in general. Petrarch,[9] in his *Trionfi*, attempts to give clear, if short, descriptions of at all events the figures of Love, of Chastity, of Death and of Fame. Others again load their allegories with inappropriate attributes.

8. poet who wrote the *Divine Comedy*   9. scholar and poet, considered the father of humanism

In the *Satires* of Vinciguerra, for example, Envy is depicted with rough, iron teeth; Gluttony as biting its own lips, and with a shock of tangled hair, the latter probably to show its indifference to all that is not meat and drink. We cannot here discuss the bad influence of these misunderstandings on the plastic arts. They, like poetry, might think themselves fortunate if allegory could be expressed by a mythological figure—by a figure which antiquity saved from absurdity—if Mars[10] might stand for war, and Diana[11] for the love of the chase.

Nevertheless art and poetry had better allegories than these to offer, and we may assume with regard to such figures of this kind as appeared in the Italian festivals, that the public required them to be clearly and vividly characteristic, since its previous training had fitted it to be a competent critic. Elsewhere, particularly at the Burgundian court, the most inexpressive figures, and even mere symbols, were allowed to pass, since to understand, or to seem to understand them, was a part of aristocratic breeding. On the occasion of the famous 'Oath of the Pheasant'[12] in the year 1454, the beautiful young horsewoman, who appears as 'Queen of Pleasure', is the only pleasing allegory. The huge dishes, with automatic or even living figures within them, are either mere curiosities or are intended to convey some clumsy moral lesson. A naked female statue guarding a live lion was supposed to represent Constantinople and its future saviour, the Duke of Burgundy. The rest, with the exception of a pantomime—Jason in Colchis[13]—seems either too recondite to be understood or to have no sense at all. Olivier himself, to whom we owe the description of the scene, appeared costumed as 'The Church', in a tower on the back of an elephant, and sang a long elegy on the victory of the unbelievers.

But although the allegorical element in the poetry, the art and the festivals of Italy is superior both in good taste and in unity of conception to what we find in other countries, yet it is not in these qualities that it is most characteristic and unique. The decisive point of superiority lay rather in the fact that, besides the personifications of abstract qualities, historical representatives of

10. Greek god of war   11. Greek goddess of the hunt   12. banquet originally held to attempt to raise a crusade to free Constantinople   13. In Greek mythology, Jason led the Argonauts to battle in Colchis.

them were introduced in great number—that both poetry and plastic art were accustomed to represent famous men and women. The *Divine Comedy*, the *Trionfi* of Petrarch, the *Amorosa visione*[14] of Boccaccio—all of them works constructed on this principle—and the great diffusion of culture which took place under the influence of antiquity, had made the nation familiar with this historical element. These figures now appeared at festivals, either individualized, as definite masks, or in groups, as characteristic attendants on some leading allegorical figure. The art of grouping and composition was thus learnt in Italy at a time when the most splendid exhibitions in other countries were made up of unintelligible symbolism or unmeaning puerilities.

14. allegory written by poet and storyteller Boccaccio

Establishing Oneself in Renaissance Society

Mark Phillips

The following except is taken from a book by Mark Phillips, professor of history at the University of British Columbia. In this book, Phillips has brought together the journals, letters, and personal documents of Marco Parenti, a silk merchant who lived in Florence during the fifteenth century. From these documents he has created a portrait of an Italian Renaissance man.

In this piece, Phillips follows Parenti's life beginning with the death of his father. After dividing up the estate between himself and his cousins, he begins to build on the fortune he has received. He does well in his dealings, and eventually moves up in social standing in Florence, surpassing his father's rank.

The economic workings of Renaissance Italy can clearly be seen, as well as an example of the new upward mobility of the society. Here is a man who took his family's prosperity and built upon its firm foundation.

A s the only son, Marco inherited Parente's house, business, and properties. His tax report of 1457 shows many continuities with his father's of a decade before—and with the whole series of declarations made by . . . Parente . . . going back to the first *catasto*, a new, more accurate form of tax assessment begun in 1427. Real estate was the most stable form of wealth. From time to time, property might be bought or sold, but most often families were either rounding out an existing holding or dividing one previously held in common. No wonder that when the boundaries of a property are described, a brother or cousin is often listed as one of the neighbors.

The house on the Via del Cocomero is a case in point. In the early *catasti* it is listed in the name of Stefano, Parente, and a nephew, Giovanni. Often such joint households were a tempo-

Mark Phillips, *The Memoir of Marco Parenti: A Life in Medici Florence*. Princeton, NJ: Princeton University Press, 1987. Copyright © 1987 by Princeton University Press. Reproduced by permission.

rary expedient following the death of the original owner; this was unlikely to have been the case here, however, since in 1433 Stefano gave his age as sixty-four, Parente's as fifty-five, and Giovanni's as thirty-one. Nonetheless, the house was eventually divided, for in 1457 Marco listed his cousins, the sons of Giovanni Parenti, as his immediate neighbors. On both sides of the household a new generation was coming into possession.

Dividing the Family Inheritance

Subdivision of the common household has sometimes been taken to signify the fragmentation of the family and the growth of individualism. Perhaps so, but since Marco and his cousins remained his closest neighbors, it would be surprising if the same family feelings—and family tensions—did not remain. It simplified matters that Marco was an only son. A more prolific family would have had to face the difficult choice of overcrowding itself in its old house or sending its sons out to find a new one. Even so, most sons chose to build, buy, or rent as close to home as possible, thus continuing to enjoy the sociability of the family and its ties to longtime neighbors.

In the countryside, where residence was not involved, arrangements were more flexible. Farms, if they were large enough, could be legally divided; more simply, the produce, already shared between the urban proprietor and the peasant who actually worked the land, could be divided once again among the common heirs. Marco listed three farms . . . in his report of 1457, all of which had been in Stefano's name in the first catasto, and in one of these his cousins were joint owners. This left Marco the possessor of a quarter of this farm's production of grain and "corn of various types." Of the two pigs, one was his, plus "a sucking pig." But, he reported, "there is no wine to be gathered at all."

A large part of Marco's inheritance came in the form of shares. . . . He declared 8,869 florins [gold currency of the period] listed in his father's name, of which some 2,170 florins had been converted to funds for the dowries of his daughters, Ginevra and Lisa. This left 6,694 florins, against which Marco pleaded for some reduction, since "there still remains Agnoletta, for whose dowry I have done nothing." Beyond this already substantial sum, Marco listed 4,765 florins inscribed in his own name and

1,000 "with stipulation" in that of Giovanni Parenti.

These were considerable holdings, even when one has taken into account the fact that the market value of the shares would have been far less than the nominal value. It is striking, too, that Marco's declared holdings on the Monte exceeded those his father had listed in 1446 and 1451. Where had this additional capital come from? The most likely explanation is that both Parente and Marco had withdrawn capital from their business and put it into the safer, less entrepreneurial form of shares in the public debt. This is suggested by another part of the declaration. "I rent," Marco wrote, "from the friars of the Charterhouse a workshop . . . for forty florins a year . . . where we used to work in silk. Now it is approximately ten years I have retained it, although I no longer exercise the trade." Apparently he did not wish to cut himself off entirely from the silk business; he chose instead to keep up his rights to the shop in order "that I not lose the use of it." But Marco had effectively entered the class that the Florentines called *scioperati*—men who kept up their guild membership for social or political reasons rather than for trade. Since unearned wealth always carries with it a certain prestige, this in some ways represented a jump in status. By withdrawing from the occupation of his uncle and father, Marco had taken their efforts to raise the family into the upper class of Florentine society one step further.

Managing the Family Fortune

It would be wrong, however, to think of Marco as rich and carefree; at least, he did not want the notaries of the catasto to think so, and he filled his declaration with lists of debts and responsibilities. In the first place there were the eight mouths he had to feed: himself, aged thirty-seven, Caterina, his wife, twenty-six; Piero, his first-born, now eight; Gostanza, aged five; Marietta, three and a half; Ginevra, two; Lisa, one; and Agnoletta, only a month old. At 200 florins apiece, these dependents amounted to a deduction of 1,600 florins.

As head of this rapidly growing family, Parenti no doubt had many expenses. He owed the banker, Bono Boni, 120 florins, but there is no indication of the purpose of the loan. A second item was the 230 florins it cost to buy a neighboring house to enlarge his own. There were smaller sums as well: 10 florins to a tailor, 5 to a workman, and 5 more to a wet nurse called Bionda di Bruno—Blonde, daughter of Brown. Finally, a deduction was allowed for properties both in the city and the countryside that had once been held in the family and had since been "alienated."

His mother's death had left Marco with responsibilities of a different sort. By her will he was charged with a series of small charitable expenses. Simona, her niece, was to have clothing to a value of 15 florins. Several convents, the prisons, and a hospital had to have 10 florins apiece, and the canons of the cathedral, the friars of Santa Croce, and the seven friars who had witnessed the will received smaller sums. Finally, the friars of San Francisco in Fiesole were endowed with 4 florins per annum so that every year in perpetuity they could say an office for the soul of the departed.

Viewed from the distance of so many years, the exact size of sums spent in honoring the dead or in enlarging a house for a growing family is not critical. These details provide a focus for the imagination and a reminder of the reassuring ordinariness of life in any period. The catasto officials, on the other hand, took a less detached view of these matters, and they filled the margins with figuring and cross-references to other declarations where Marco's might be corroborated. When all was added in, they figured Parenti's total wealth as 3,689 florins, against which they allowed deductions of 1,837 florins, leaving a taxable "surplus" of 1,852 florins. Florentines paid a standard rate of .5 percent, a figure that seems remarkably low until one remembers that it is based on total wealth, not yearly income, and that it could be levied as often as the government saw the need. In all, including a small head tax, Marco was assessed fi.9 s.11 d.3.

By itself the figure is not very helpful, but fortunately, the records for 1457 are unusually complete and a table showing the distribution of tax assessments has been worked out that allows us a reasonably accurate guide to Parenti's economic status. In that year there were 317 households that were assessed between 5 and 10 florins, representing approximately 4 percent of the 7,636 households paying taxes. In all, 97 percent of Florentine households paid 10 florins or less; only 227 households paid more. In short, Marco, with his assessment of a little over 9½ florins, probably stood just outside of the top 3 percent of taxpayers.

Backed by these statistics, our estimate of Marco's economic status seems fairly secure. In 1457, however, Marco was still a young man and his responsibilities were considerable. It would be a reasonable guess that his income at that time was relatively low, a suspicion that can be confirmed by checking figures for other years. Marco listed his own and his father's previous assessments at the beginning of his 1469 declaration:

1427.	Stefano and			
	Parenti di Giovanni Parenti	fi. 19	s. 11	d. 10
1451.	Parente di Giovanni Parenti	23	5	—
1457.	Marco di Parente Parenti	9	11	3
1468.	Marco	17	1	9

To this list we can also add the assessment found at the end of the 1469 declaration itself—fi. 19 s.7 d.3—and the much reduced figure for 1480 of fi.9 s.2 d.6.

Parenti's declaration for 1457 provides a rather low estimate of his financial status when compared to the figures for subsequent years. It seems clear that although Marco never equaled Parente's highest assessment, over the course of a lifetime he did not lag too far behind his father. There had been some fluctuations, but these were natural to the life cycle of families. Marco was able to maintain the family fortune and see a new generation safely launched.

By mid-century—the years of Marco's early manhood—the Parenti had found a place in the Florentine upper class. In two generations they had risen out of the ranks of the artisans and "new citizens" for whom Giovanni Parenti had been a spokesman, into the class Giovanni and his companions had opposed. In this new status the Parenti never achieved real prominence or power, but at least they had arrived. Thus in 1472, when Benedetto Dei, the crankiest of Florentine private chroniclers, compiled a list of leading Florentine families, whose presence was an ornament to the city and a "confusion to our enemies," the Parenti found a place.

The commercial energies of his uncle and father had lifted the family into this new niche, but it was Marco who inherited the benefits. First among them was the marriage to Caterina Strozzi. Marco's letters of the time show his pride in being connected to this old and prominent house, and in later years, as the Strozzi brothers rebuilt their fortunes, the connection became more prestigious. Equally, Marco was still a young man in 1454 when he was selected to the Signoria [ruling class], an honor for which his father had waited until the end of his life. In education, too, Marco seems to have been privileged beyond his parents, and he became part of a circle of well-educated and socially prominent young men.

In a sense, though, the most notable of the privileges Marco inherited was the freedom to withdraw from the silk business that had created his family's prosperity. Of this important decision nothing is said either in his letters or in his private record book, but its significance seems clear. Marco was then a young man, recently and advantageously married. His father, nearing the end of his life, presumably was no longer able to direct the business, which would have to survive on the energies of the young—energies that were directed instead to establishing a household and raising a family, to the first steps of a political career, and to the literary and political interests of Marco's circle.

Agriculture and Country Life

Peter Laven

Though the city and the urban life of the Renaissance usually garner the most attention, the country played a large part in developing the economic fortunes of the time. Agriculture in Italy was a major source of income, and the control of lands that surrounded the urban centers was a high priority.

In the following selection, Peter Laven, research fellow at the University of Kent in Canterbury, England, provides an overview of life in the Italian countryside. The crops produced at the time were many and varied. From livestock to grain to grapes, the fertile countryside provided consistent production and income.

It was not only the wealthy landowners who benefited from the bounty. The agriculture industry employed many as crops were planted, fields tended, and harvests brought in. Roads and canals were also built to transport the goods. The thriving economy of the countryside helped fuel the boom that drove the Renaissance.

In a period when the rest of Europe was suffering from an economic depression and a decline in population, northern Italy and especially Milan was adapting itself not only to survive, but indeed to expand. The opportunity may have been fortuitous, but the method, if self-interested, was calculated and original. The church was rich in land accumulated haphazardly from the bequests of the devout, largely in the interests of their departed souls. What it lacked in the later Middle Ages was money, which in a developing money economy it needed more and more urgently, particularly since it was so difficult to enforce the services due to it from its scattered peasants and was having to go over to the employment of wage-earners. To get money the churches were forced to lease their lands. Investors—feudal lords, successful city merchants, soldiers or lawyers, shopkeepers or arti-

Peter Laven, *Renaissance Italy: 1464–1534*. New York: G.P. Putnam's Sons, 1966. Copyright © 1966 by Peter Laven. All rights reserved. Reproduced by permission of the Literary Estate of Peter Laven.

sans—saw their chance. A form of contract including improvement clauses was used. It required at the expiry of the lease that the lessor make good money used by the tenant for improving the property. Failing this the tenant was able to repeat the lease under the same conditions as before. Seldom could the Church, owing to its cash shortage, meet the first alternative. Accordingly speculators got hold of land made increasingly valuable by improvement—at very low rents, which were even relatively reduced during periods of rising prices. These speculators aimed at gathering together blocks of land, and thus they altered fundamentally the pattern of landownership, the scattered possessions that had characterised the past. Even the old feudal nobility tended to consolidate much of its property. Consolidation had several attractions. Improvements such as the provision of irrigation ditches or farm buildings were far more economical if they were to serve a compact stretch of land. The tenants, virtually the new owners of the land, were capitalistic speculators aiming to produce for the biggest and most profitable markets. They were behind the big dairy farms, the large-scale woad[1] production, the experiment in rice. To farm for a commercial market, everything had to be streamlined. Labour charges and equipment costs were lower, marketing facilities were more efficient, if production was centralised. Ultimately, despite early fifteenth-century ducal legislation forbidding it, the Church in return for a slight rise in the rent granted perpetual leases. The new owners usually did not live on the land. They sublet it on contracts of *mezzadria*[2] extremely favourable to themselves or used hired labour to work it for them. Sometimes they acquired the land from the Church by exchanging for it other land, not of equal extent but of a real value equal to the absurdly low nominal value of the land in question. Land acquired one way or another was often resold at enormous profit. The dukes—in the first place the Visconti[3] later the Sforza[4]—were generally in favour of what was going on. They built roads which encouraged the commercial exploitation of the land, but which at the same time helped them to control the feudal lords. With the increase of rural works on canals, farm-

---

1. herb used to create blue dye   2. a sharecropper contract that involved at least twenty to twenty-five families   3. ruling family in Milan   4. ruling family in Milan

buildings and so forth, and with the revival of the land, the countryside and the villages were repopulated and rural industries returned and made possible the dispersal of the unemployed or discontented to perhaps a more satisfied existence in the country. A new class of supporters of the dukes was being fostered, men whose vision could only be realised if the whole weight of the community were harnessed to it. The dukes won them by developing the canal system which provided cheap transport and by extending the drainage and irrigation networks of Lombardy to their advantage. Farms became more efficient; the duchy more prosperous. Finally, by taxing the Church, the dukes speeded up the process of capitalists acquiring Church lands, for the Church's need for money was accordingly aggravated.

The process of capitalistic exploitation was ultimately self-defeating. Sometimes the turnover of land at a profit became more important than the use of the land itself. At others the money-making urgency did not survive many generations and the speculator of his descendant became the country gentleman, enjoying rather than exploiting his possessions. By the end of the fifteenth century the Church had little more land to filch, and the properties of small owners had fast disappeared into the consolidated properties of the big landowners. As the sixteenth century progressed the landowners had to look outside Milanese territories to the mountains behind Bergamo to find workers willing or available to accept unfavourable *mezzadria* contracts. Then with the Counter-Reformation[5] the Church began to acquire land anew. No longer was it on the defensive. No longer had it to surrender its land to city speculators. Now the economy was dominated by the demands of Hapsburg[6] Spain; and a régime in which Church, landlord and foreigner held sway was doomed to lose the dynamism formerly bestowed upon it by the expedients of capitalistic enterprise.

A Variety of Crops

To the west of the duchy of Milan were the small states of Asti and Montferrat and the Piedmontese[7] territories of Savoy. Much

---

5. series of reactions of the Catholic Church against the Protestant Reformation   6. ruling family in Western Europe from the thirteenth to the twentieth century   7. in the region of the Piedmont Mountains in northern Italy

the same pattern of development took place here as in Milan. Irrigation allowed the change to cattle farming, and rice culture was developed somewhat later in the sixteenth century than in the Lombardy. Local flax supported the fustian industry of Chieri, which like other north Italian examples of the industry suffered from the competition of south Germany. The Piedmontese silk production, which flourished in the fifteenth century, was severely hit by the wars in the first part of the sixteenth century, and it was only under the active encouragement of Emmanuel Philibert[8] of Savoy that a silk industry restored the successful growth of the mulberry. At the same time, hemp cultivation continued to expand, despite the presence of French troops, and by 1529 huge exports were recorded, while behind the juncture of Alp and Apennine the vineyards of the Langhe bore a prosperous and well-famed wine industry.

The duchy of Mantua, pushed back by Venice from the shores of Lake Garda and watered by the Mincio and the Po, was famous for its horses, and to feed them it grew large amounts of spelt and oats, although by the second half of the sixteenth century wheat took up over half of the cultivated lands of the duchy. Sheep farming was encouraged by the privileged position of the woollen industry at Mantua, and the north Italian process of replacing sheep with cattle was checked, even though transhumant cattle from Venice encroached upon Mantuan territory. That wolves were still a menace to the livestock of Mantua perhaps indicates the limits of man's control over his environment at this stage of the history of northern Italy. Ferrara, consisting of the technically papal state of Ferrara and the no less technically imperial fief of Modena, was also mainly concerned with the production of wheat. This was actively encouraged by Borso d'Este, duke in the third quarter of the fifteenth century, and by Ercole II, who inherited the duchy in 1534. But in the meantime, even in bad years, Ferrara was always sufficiently supplied with corn, while in good years as much as two-thirds of the crop was used for export, with Venice the chief customer, Finally, the sodden meadows of Ferrara like the rest of the Po Valley saw a growing cattle industry, and Ferrara cheese was well known beyond the confines of the duchy. . . .

8. duke of Savoy

Rice came later to the Terraferma than to the duchy of Milan. Its introduction was under urban influence and ricefields consequently were developed near the towns. This produced ill-feeling between official and landowner: the one in the interests of public health trying to enforce laws keeping the rice swamps at a distance from the town populations, the other in the interests of profit continuing to grow rice on the city outskirts. In the 1520s such a conflict was aroused on account of ricefields around Verona. Furthermore the innovation of rice was to the detriment of local wheat and beef production. To check the decline the government of Venice in 1529 fixed a quota of 1,000 beef cattle to be provided by Verona annually. This did not alter things and a quarter of a century later Verona was pleading that it was impossible to provide so many head of cattle. In spite of the official attitude the growing of rice continued to expand in Venetian territories until it reached a peak in the last decades of the seventeenth century. . . .

Agriculture in Venice

Venetian farming was much more varied than has hitherto been indicated. Sheep-farming was not limited to the far north-west of the state, but followed the valleys and foothills right around the south-eastern regions of the Alps. Likewise vineyards were to be found terraced on the shores of Garda or at Chioggia, on the hills about Padua or on the islands of the lagoon. Pig-farming was important in the wheat country of Friuli, where the hams were reputedly of good quality, whilst in the south the Polesina di Rovigo sent its poultry to Venice. Later in the sixteenth century maize was introduced, but it was not before the eighteenth century that it began to dominate the landscape. Hemp too was an important crop of the Terraferma, partly answering the needs of the shipbuilding industry at Venice. Timber for the ships was floated down from the Dolomites, for instance on the Adige, to be towed from south of Chioggia into the lagoon, and firewood was brought to Venice from Istria. But the use of timber was reckless, and Venice was confronted with a crippling wood famine by the end of the sixteenth century.

For long rich patricians and citizens of Venice had bought properties on the mainland in territories which had not yet been brought under Venetian control. As the frontiers of Venice advanced they continued to buy land, cashing in on the sequestrated properties of uncooperative landlords or on their loss of prosperity resulting from changed political conditions. As civil governors or military captains in subject territories, the Venetian patricians had every occasion to buy up land on very favourable terms, and they did not fail to do so. The property gathered together in this way was fairly scattered, because the opportunities to buy did not necessarily give the purchaser the chance to accumulate large consolidated blocks. But with the vigorous reclamation of the sixteenth century, estates emerged as considerable units, although one owner might have such blocks in three or four different districts. There was also great competition for the control of mills, and very often a mill would be divided into three or four shares. Despite the considerable possession of landed property by the rich Venetians, little seems to have been done to work or improve it until Venice had extricated herself from the terrible consequences of the wars following the League of Cambrai.[9] This was also the case with consolidated blocks of land acquired by monasteries. Perhaps in the 1520s, when the first real opportunity arose to compensate for trade losses to the Portuguese by developing the Terraferma, attention was turned to the land. Soon the patrician would learn the delights of the countryside and adorn his estates with a villa, perhaps built by Palladio.[10] Certainly the second half of the century and the first half of the next saw a great expansion of such settlement and the merchant nobility cast itself in the mould of a country squirearchy.

9. alliance of most of the southern European states against Venice   10. architect who first developed the villa style and coined the name

Health and Education

CHAPTER
2

Chapter Preface

The beginning of the Renaissance saw the development and establishment of civic pride and duty. Towns and villages took pride in how clean their streets were and how many of their students completed their schooling. Two of the earliest influences that brought about these changes seem, on the surface, to be very different, yet both played a significant role in shaping the communities of the Renaissance.

The emergence of scholars and teachers bent on reviving the study of the classic works of the Greek and Roman philosophers was one influence. This study led to the development of a new philosophy called humanism, which focused on people's interests, achievements, and values rather than on theology or science. The humanists nurtured learning and the arts, and sought to advance the condition of man by improving the culture and society in which he lived.

These humanist scholars and their teachings began to change how education was viewed. In the new social order, in which an individual was not locked into a certain class, the concept of education as a means to better one's life and improve one's standing took hold. Once limited to the wealthy and those serving in the church, education was now seen as a wise and noble path for all citizens living in and around towns and cities. Schools and universities were built and teachers hired. Scholarships were established for poorer students to attend universities, with even the smallest towns sending students. Education was seen as a way to better the community, to bring glory and power and to improve the quality of an area.

The second influence, the Black Plague, swept through Italy and all of Europe with a vengeance in 1347. Before it ended in 1351, it had killed between one-third and one-half of the population of Europe. As a result, public attitudes toward health and issues of city planning changed radically during and after the outbreak of the plague. Health boards were formed, regulations were put in place to deal with sewage and sanitation, and the concept of a clean, healthy town was born. This was a major change from the medieval way of approaching the issue, which was to toss all waste out the window or in the street. The specter of the plague convinced the people that spending money to improve the condition of their town was a wise investment. Sewer systems were designed and implemented. Public water sources were established and regulated. Rubbish removal was enforced. The cities and towns of the Renaissance worked to provide a clean, healthy environment for their citizens.

These two separate, very different events had a very similar effect on the people of the Renaissance. Each, in its own way, united cities, towns, and regions together as they never had been before. Instead of a military alliance or an economic pact, these areas were now united to defeat the plague and to attempt to prevent it from returning. They were united in their efforts to provide education to their children, both rich and poor alike. Small villages, large cities, different families and political allies now had something to unite them, to bring them together with a common goal. This fact, coupled with the recent economic improvement that gave these areas the means to carry out such goals, brought about the development of the concept of civic responsibility extending beyond one's family and fortune. Now, in addition to seeking to advance in society, the good of the community became a priority for the men and women of the Renaissance.

Attitudes Toward Health and Cleanliness

Douglas Biow

Douglas Biow is a professor of Italian at the University of Texas at Austin. He has written several books and articles on the Renaissance, including *Doctors, Ambassadors, Secretaries: Humanism and Professions in Renaissance Italy* and *Mirabile Dictu: Representations of the Marvelous in Medieval and Renaissance Epic.* In this piece, Biow uses the words of one of Florence's most ardent defenders to show the heightened level of awareness of cleanliness that existed during the Renaissance. He then discusses the effect of the Black Plague on attitudes and actions taken to ensure public health.

> The Italians of the day lived in the belief that they were more cleanly than other nations. There are in fact general reasons which speak rather for than against this claim. Cleanliness is indispensable to our modern notion of social perfection, which was developed in Italy earlier than elsewhere.
> —Jacob Burckhardt,[1] *The Civilization of the Renaissance in Italy*

In 1527, The "most illustrious" (*chiarissimo*) Marco Foscari, ambassador to Florence—then the Republic of Machiavelli[2] and Michelangelo—returned home and delivered . . . [a] report to his senate of fellow noblemen. . . .

Readily apparent in the Venetian ambassador's report is the nobleman's well-bred, overly refined disdain for anyone who holds a trade. In this particular case, however, what is so shocking for Foscari is that the leaders of the Florentine government actually roll up their sleeves and work with their lessers; their children do the same—and they do this publicly, for all to witness (*pubblicamente*). Indeed, it would almost seem that the Florentine leaders make a point of flaunting their free association

---

1. nineteenth-century historian who specialized in the Renaissance   2. political philosopher who wrote *The Prince*

Douglas Biow, "The Politics of Cleanliness in Northern Renaissance Italy," *Symposium*, vol. 50, Summer 1996, pp. 75–86. Copyright © 1996 by the Helen Dwight Reid Educational Foundation, published by Heldref Publications, 1319 18th St. NW, Washington, DC 20036-1802. Reproduced by permission.

with the workers whom they have hired. For the Venetian Foscari, this is not a well-ordered state, the government of noblemen, but a republic of parvenus in which all the elements are physically enmeshed in "vile labors" (*vili esercizi*) with men who are not just base but, in a word, "filthy" (*sporchi*).

Nothing so aptly captures the Venetian ambassador's disdain as the image of filth that he attributes to these Florentine men engaged in mechanical and manual labors, working side by side with their hired help, performing with their own hands tasks otherwise relegated to "dirty men" (*uomini sporchi*). It is one thing to call men vile (*vili, vilissimi*) as the Venetian ambassador repeatedly and emphatically does, for vile connotes low, the lesser rank of society, an accepted category in political discourse. But to call these men filthy (*sporchi*) is at once to raise the possibility of contamination. Filth may spread, and for Foscari the entire web of Florentine society seems to have become entangled (*intricat[o]*) in its own mire. Physical contact with dirty men by the men who lead society may well create a society of dirty men. These Florentines have gotten their hands dirty, and in so doing they have perhaps inexcusably dirtied the state.

Another View: Florence as the Model of Cleanliness

Foscari's frank, though unmistakably biased, report will prove a fitting point of contrast with and introduction to a very different description of Florentine society, a description that is not the work of an outsider peering in, an ambassador only too happy to return home. Rather, it is a famous description composed by Leonardo Bruni,[3] an Aretine[4] but nonetheless an insider, a man who occupied a central role in Florentine politics as chancellor of the Republic and . . . the great promoter of Florentine civic humanism. Indeed, in his glowing panegyric to the city of Florence, *Laudatio Florentinae Urbis*[5] written nearly a century before Foscari's report, Leonardo Bruni states that he does not know how to begin to talk about such a wondrous city. Only after a series of calculated rhetorical disclaimers does Bruni at last accept the

---

3. humanist, scholar, and historian   4. from the city of Aretino, where Bruni was born
5. *Praise for the City of Florence*

arduous chore at hand. So many features of the city are praise-worthy, he declares, it is almost impossible to choose: the power of Florence, its wealth, institutions, customs, history, beauty, sumptuous palaces, location, splendor. When Bruni finally chooses, however, when he suddenly seizes upon the "most apt and logical place to begin," he places an incessant, indeed an al-most obsessive, emphasis on the city's crystalline cleanliness. For Bruni, in fact, cleanliness earmarks Florence from the outset as a truly exceptional city:

> . . . every other city is so dirty that the filth created during the night is seen in the early morning by the population and tram-pled under foot in the streets. Really can one think of anything worse than this? Even if there were a thousand palaces in such a city and inexhaustible wealth, even if it possessed an infinite pop-ulation, still I would always condemn that city as a stinking place and not think highly of it. . . . Hence filthy cities that may in other respects be very good can never be considered to be beautiful.

Predictably, of course, Florence is a swan of a different color:

> Indeed, it seems to me that Florence is so clean and neat that no other city could be cleaner. Surely this city is unique and singu-lar in all the world because you will find here nothing that is dis-gusting to the eye, offensive to the nose, or filthy under foot. The great diligence of its inhabitants ensures and provides that all filth is removed from the streets, so you see only what brings plea-sure and joy to the senses. Therefore, in its splendor Florence probably surpasses all the cities of the world, and, moreover, in its elegance it is without doubt far ahead of all the cities that ex-ist now and all that ever will. Indeed, such unparalleled cleanli-ness must be incredible to those who have never seen Florence, for we who live here are amazed daily and will never take for granted this fine quality of Florence. Now what is more mar-velous in a populous city than never to have to worry about filth in the streets? Moreover, however big a rainstorm, it cannot pre-vent your walking through the city with dry feet since almost be-fore it falls the rainwater is taken away by appropriately placed gutters. Hence, the cleanliness and dryness that you find only in the rooms of private palaces in other cities, you find in the squares and streets of Florence.

. . . It is not long, however, before we realize that Bruni's aes-thetics and rhetoric are of a larger political strategy. In comparing Florence with other cities, for example, Bruni asserts that elsewhere

> . . . it is very important that in other cities a tourist should not stay too long. In those cities, what they have to show is all publicly displayed and is placed (as it were) on the outward bark. Whoever comes into these cities is seen as a stranger; but if these tourists leave the well-frequented places and try to examine the interiors as well as the exteriors of the buildings, there will be nothing to confirm their first impressions. Indeed, instead of houses they will find only small huts, and behind the exterior decorations only filth. But the beauty of Florence cannot be appreciated unless seen from the inside.

Elsewhere, according to Bruni, public display serves to mask the mire within the private worlds. In Florence, however, private space and public space begin to overlap. That, of course, does not mean that private property becomes public property in Bruni's *Laudatio*, as it does, for example, in [Sir Thomas] More's *Utopia*.[6] No one more than Bruni broadcasts the virtue of private wealth. No one is more proud and boastful than Bruni about the magnificence of private palaces in Florence. What Bruni is questioning, however, is the system that contains such ornament, magnificence, and wealth, just as [Friedrich] Engels[7] conversely questions the validity of capitalist society by analyzing "the planning of a city whereby the 'dirty' was made invisible to the bourgeoisie." A city may be as wealthy as Florence but not clean, as magnificent but not clean, as beautiful but not clean, externally praiseworthy but in the interior shamefully filthy. The notion of hiding and disclosing, of the interior and exterior, is therefore pivotal in Bruni's use of cleanliness. On the surface, to be clean is to highlight a particular feature, to quite literally show off; but to be clean within signifies that one has nothing to hide. Bruni invites us to see Florence from within, and in so doing he is inviting us to inspect the system itself. Wealth may divide the Florentine world into the haves and the have-nots, but cleanliness is the common currency that penetrates all levels of society. When moving from the lush quarters of a magnificent private palace to the wide open arena of the public square, Bruni's hy-

6. book about a fictional island described as having an ideal society   7. German socialist

pothetical visitor is expected to find everywhere the same caring concern for cleanliness. In both instances cleanliness is as much a civic virtue as it is a private virtue; it is as openly apparent as it is tucked away in the hidden interiors of houses; it is as much a characteristic of the poor as the rich. Far from being the privilege of any particular social group, cleanliness is one of the great homogenizing elements in the city's physical and social structure. For the civic-minded Bruni, cleanliness is the visible guarantee that the system works, and therefore becomes in a very real way a metaphor for the system itself. . . .

Cleanliness and Help

Now whereas civic humanism may help to explain Bruni's hyperbolic emphasis upon Florence as the cleanest of cities, it is also true that throughout northern Italy the social virtue of cleanliness had gradually become an eminent concern, be it on a private or public scale, with individual or civic ramifications. The Black Death[8] and the subsequent outbreaks that ravaged the cities and countryside from time to time contributed to fostering and improving a civic sense of hygiene. During the pandemic of the Black Plague, two temporary health boards came into being for the first time in Italy, one in Florence and the other in Venice, and both helped to ensure, among other measures, that their cities be kept clean: "streets were to be cleaned, garbage collected, sewers emptied, and the sale of meat and fruits strictly regulated.". . .

Initially, these health boards were temporarily established only after outbreaks of plague. Eventually, over the course of two hundred years, they became permanent institutions. Milan led the way in the beginning of the fifteenth century, Venice in January 1486, and Florence in June 1527. According to [Carlo] Cipolla[9] "by the second half of the sixteenth century all major Italian cities had permanent Health Boards." More impressive, perhaps, is the fact that "by the last quarter of the fifteenth century the appointment of Health Offices as an emergency measure was a common fact even in small, remote villages." Unlike any other European country, Italy had institutionalized a preventive stance against the

---

8. plague that hit Europe in the early fourteenth century   9. renowned historian of the Renaissance

outbreak of plague, both in the form of permanent boards in large cities and emergency measures in small towns.

Though often consulted, physicians did not play a large role in the policy-making of the health boards. Following Galen,[10] the prevailing medical explanation for the plague, as for all diseases, was that corruption of the air occurred during periods of pestilence. Fetid odors carrying the disease should therefore be avoided through the removal of filth. Gentile da Foligno, a famous physician who aided Pistoia in setting up sanitary measures during the outbreak of the Black Plague, declared that filth accumulating on the ground and stagnant waters proliferated the disease. Generally speaking, all physicians agreed that one should flee from fetid places; though it was recommended to often wash one's hands with vinegar, bathing was ill-advised because it opened the pores to the disease. . . .

Clearly the medical profession played a role in implementing sanitary measures. It was, however, largely due to the perceived, and not medically reasoned, connection between filth and the plague that ordinances for improving the sanitary conditions of the cities ever saw the light of day. Indeed, as Cipolla notes, "the rise and development of the Health Boards and of related health legislation were not so much the brainchild of the medical profession as they were the products of the administrative talents of the Italian Renaissance society." Rules stipulating how people were to "converse" (*conversare*) and the extent of contact that could be permitted became eminent concerns of the legislators since the time of the Black Plague, because [they became] increasingly important with each new outbreak. To the point of defying even the medical opinion of the time, the officials considered the plague to be highly contagious. Beginning in the mid-1400s, *lazzaretti*[11] were operating in all major cities, the first appearing in Venice. As early as the 1370s, Bernabo Visconti[12] reenacted desperate sanitary laws in the conviction that the plague was contagious; Giangaleazzo[13] closed the city gates, thus quarantining the city; and Filippo Maria[14] went so far as to actu-

10. Greek physician who was viewed as the ultimate authority on medicine   11. quarantine stations for plague victims   12. ruler of Milan   13. nephew of Bernabo Visconti, ruled Milan after having his uncle arrested   14. son of Giangaleazzo; ruled Milan after his brother was assassinated

ally wall up the undiseased with the sick. During the outbreak of plague, measures of control included banning of public processions and festive gatherings, the closing of schools, and limiting the number of people who could attend burials.

Perhaps some of the most significant factors were measures taken during the periods when there was no pestilence at all. In their attempt to prevent the spread of disease, the health boards throughout northern Italy had decided to monitor the flow of traffic between cities and towns. As a result, from the second half of the fifteenth century, health passes came into use. This meant that neither person nor merchandise would be admitted to a given place without a document issued by recognized authority. In its more elaborate form, the pass had to certify the identity of the holder, the country from which he had come, the fact that he had been there for at least a certain period, and that at the moment of departure he had been in good health and was not a possible contact.

In short, though public ordinances had already existed in abundance prior to the outbreak of the Black Plague, these health boards, from the vantage point of a centralized bureaucracy and authority, could now pursue with increased vigor such preexisting legislation concerning the cleaning of streets, the disposal of garbage, the drainage of sewers, the control of food sold, and the inspection of goods brought into the city.

Along with the enforcement of previous legislation came added restrictions. Within ten years of becoming a permanent institution, the health board of Venice began to follow through with more decisive regulations in order to clean the city. During the reign of Cosimo I[15] and Ferdinando I,[16] the city of Florence provided for and maintained an elaborate, if not always efficient, sewage system. Ferrara during the time of Ariosto[17] enacted rigorous reforms in its intent to control the sanitary conditions of the city. In Milan, from 1493 on, broad domains of public interest increasingly fell under the jurisdiction of the health board; in 1590, the board finally compiled an elaborate ordinance composed of forty-six articles which had permanent validity, and

15. duke of Florence from 1537–1569; grand duke of Tuscany from 1569 to 1574   16. son of Cosimo I and grand duke from 1574 to 1609   17. poet and citizen of Ferrara

aimed not at times of contagion but at 'salubrious times.' The ordinance was repeatedly published at almost regular intervals and it dealt with the cleanliness of the streets, the sanitary conditions of private dwellings, the disposal of refuse, the collection of dung, the discharges of tanneries. Special attention was generally devoted to the quality of foodstuffs and the hygienic conditions under which they were sold.

Now of course all this legislation does not mean that the cities and towns of northern Italy were startlingly clean during the Renaissance, nor, for that matter, that they were necessarily cleaner than they were in the Middle Ages. What all this legislation does indicate, however, is a heightened awareness of the standards of public hygiene. Not surprisingly, standards of public behavior in the late Renaissance, that is to say, manners, seemed to have developed along analogous lines. No less surprising, for that matter, is that this heightened awareness also parallels the increasingly disdainful attitude of the elite toward those who occupied mechanical trades. Indeed, just as cleanliness was institutionalized through law and socially divulgated through etiquette treatises such as [cleric and poet] Della Casa's *Galateo*, so too the representation of cleanliness had become politicized through the legislation of the elite. By the sixteenth century, throughout much of northern Italy, legislation explicitly excluded anyone connected with a mechanical trade, any of the *"villisimi uomini e sporchi,"* to borrow the Venetian ambassador's phrase, from political activity. From Bruni's Florentine mercantile world to Della Casa's Renaissance with its rising nobility, the elite were progressively distancing themselves and sometimes perceiving that distance through the image of filth. To remain pure, clean, and uncontaminated in the late sixteenth century was no longer just a civic social virtue (as it had been for Bruni), but for the aristocracy gradually solidifying and legitimizing its power, it had become a legal obligation as well.

The Plague in Italy

Marchione di Coppo Stefani

Little is known of Marchione di Coppo Stefani, the writer of the Florentine chronicle from which this article is excerpted. He was born in Florence in 1336 and wrote his journal from the late 1370s to the early 1380s.

In this section of the chronicle, he tells of the outbreak of plague that hit the city in 1348. He recounts the horror of watching so many die and dealing with sick family and friends. He describes the reaction of many to flee those in need and to escape to the countryside in an attempt to avoid infection.

The plague not only had personal effects; it changed the culture and economy of the day as well. The daily rhythms of life were disrupted and the economy severely hampered as businesses closed down and items related to treating the plague and disposing of the dead became extremely expensive. This account shows how devastating the results of the plague were and how profoundly it affected Italy.

Concerning a Mortality in the City of Florence in Which Many People Died

In the year of the Lord 1348 there was a very great pestilence in the city and district of Florence. It was of such a fury and so tempestuous that in houses in which it took hold previously healthy servants who took care of the ill died of the same illness. Almost none of the ill survived past the fourth day. Neither physicians nor medicines were effective. Whether because these illnesses were previously unknown or because physicians had not previously studied them, there seemed to be no cure. There was such a fear that no one seemed to know what to do. When it took hold in a house it often happened that no one remained who had not died. And it was not just that men and women died, but even sentient animals died. Dogs, cats, chickens, oxen, donkeys, sheep showed the same symptoms and died of the

Marchione di Coppo Stefani, *Cronaca Fiorentina*. Rerum Italicarum Scriptores, vol. 30, edited by Niccolo Rodolico. Citta di Castello: 1903–1913.

same disease. And almost none, or very few, who showed these symptoms, were cured. The symptoms were the following: a bubo[1] in the groin, where the thigh meets the trunk; or a small swelling under the armpit; sudden fever; spitting blood and saliva (and no one who spit blood survived it). It was such a frightful thing that when it got into a house, as was said, no one remained. Frightened people abandoned the house and fled to another. Those in town fled to villages. Physicians could not be found because they had died like the others. And those who could be found wanted vast sums in hand before they entered the house. And when they did enter, they checked the pulse with face turned away. They inspected the urine from a distance and with something odoriferous under their nose. Child abandoned the father, husband the wife, wife the husband, one brother the other, one sister the other. In all the city there was nothing to do but to carry the dead to a burial. And those who died had neither confessor nor other sacraments. And many died with no one looking after them. And many died of hunger because when someone took to bed sick, another in the house, terrified, said to him: "I'm going for the doctor." Calmly walking out the door, the other left and did not return again. Abandoned by people, without food, but accompanied by fever, they weakened. There were many who pleaded with their relatives not to abandon them when night fell. But [the relatives] said to the sick person, "So that during the night you did not have to awaken those who serve you and who work hard day and night, take some sweetmeats,[2] wine or water. They are here on the bedstead by your head; here are some blankets." And when the sick person had fallen asleep, they left and did not return. If it happened that he was strengthened by the food during the night he might be alive and strong enough to get to the window. If the street was not a major one, he might stand there a half hour before anyone came by. And if someone did pass by, and if he was strong enough that he could be heard when he called out to them, sometimes there might be a response and sometimes not, but there was no help. No one, or few, wished to enter a house where anyone was sick, nor did they even want to deal with

1. a swollen gland   2. candies or cakes

those healthy people who came out of a sick person's house. And they said to them: "He is stupefied, do not speak to him!" saying further: "He has it because there is a bubo in his house." They call the swelling a bubo. Many died unseen. So they remained in their beds until they stank. And the neighbors, if there were any, having smelled the stench, placed them in a shroud and sent them for burial. The house remained open and yet there was no one daring enough to touch anything because it seemed that things remained poisoned and that whoever used them picked up the illness.

At every church, or at most of them, they dug deep trenches, down to the waterline, wide and deep, depending on how large the parish was. And those who were responsible for the dead carried them on their backs in the night in which they died and threw them into the ditch, or else they paid a high price to those who would do it for them. The next morning, if there were many [bodies] in the trench, they covered them over with dirt. And then more bodies were put on top of them, with a little more dirt over those; they put layer on layer just like one puts layers of cheese in a lasagna.

Economic and Cultural Impact of the Plague

The *beccamorti* [literally, vultures] who provided their service, were paid such a high price that many were enriched by it. Many died from [carrying away the dead], some rich, some after earning just a little, but high prices continued. Servants, or those who took care of the ill, charged from one to three florins[3] per day and the cost of things grew. The things that the sick ate, sweetmeats and sugar, seemed priceless. Sugar cost from three to eight florins per pound. And other confections cost similarly. Capons and other poultry were very expensive and eggs cost between twelve and twenty-four pence each; and he was blessed who could find three per day even if he searched the entire city. Finding wax was miraculous. A pound of wax would have gone up more than a florin if there had not been a stop put [by the communal government] to the vain ostentation that the Florentines always

3. a gold coin that was the common currency of Florence during the Renaissance

make [over funerals]. Thus it was ordered that no more than two large candles could be carried [in any funeral]. Churches had no more than a single bier which usually was not sufficient. Spice dealers and *beccamorti* sold biers, burial palls, and cushions at very high prices. Dressing in expensive woolen cloth as is customary in [mourning] the dead, that is, in a long cloak, with mantle and veil that used to cost women three florins, climbed in price to thirty florins and would have climbed to 100 florins had the custom of dressing in expensive cloth not been changed. The rich dressed in modest woolens, those not rich sewed [clothes] in linen. Benches on which the dead were placed cost like the heavens and still the benches were only a hundredth of those needed. Priests were not able to ring bells as they would have liked. Concerning that, [the government] issued ordinances discouraging the sounding of bells, sale of burial benches, and limiting expenses. They could not sound bells, sell benches, nor cry out announcements because the sick hated to hear of this and it discouraged the healthy as well. Priests and friars went [to serve] the rich in great multitudes and they were paid such high prices that they all got rich. And therefore [the authorities] ordered that one could not have more than a prescribed number [of clerics] of the local parish church. And the prescribed number of friars was six. All fruits with a nut at the center, like unripe plums and unhusked almonds, fresh broadbeans, figs and every useless and unhealthy fruit, were forbidden entrance into the city. Many processions, including those with relics and the painted tablet of Santa Maria Impruneta, went through the city crying out "Mercy" and praying and then they came to a stop in the piazza of the Priors. There they made peace concerning important controversies, injuries and deaths. This [pestilence] was a matter of such great discouragement and fear that men gathered together in order to take some comfort in dining together. And each evening one of them provided dinner to ten companions and the next evening they planned to eat with one of the others. And sometimes if they planned to eat with a certain one he had no meal prepared because he was sick. Or if the host had made dinner for the ten, two or three were missing. Some fled to villas, others to villages in order to get a change of air. Where there had been no [pestilence], there they carried it; if it was already there, they caused it to increase. None of the guilds in Florence was working. All the shops were shut, taverns closed; only the apothecaries and the churches remained open. If you went outside, you found almost no one. And many good and rich men

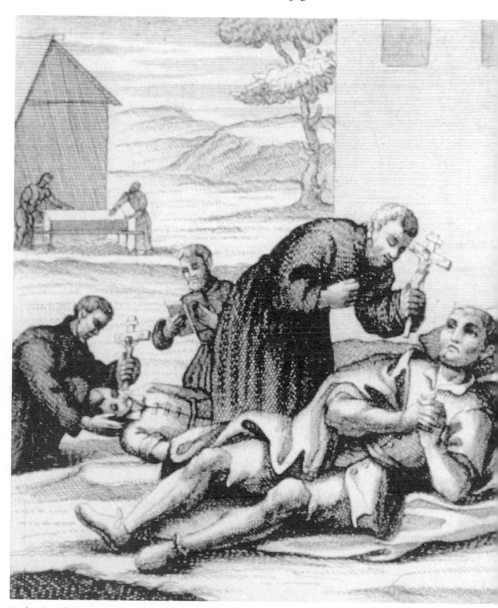

Priests administer last rites to plague victims. The plague outbreak in 1348 devastated Italy and profoundly altered society.

were carried from home to church on a pall by four *beccamorti* and one tonsured[4] clerk who carried the cross. Each of them wanted a florin. This mortality enriched apothecaries, doctors, poultry vendors, *beccamorti*, and greengrocers who sold poultices of mallow, nettles, mercury and other herbs necessary to draw off the infirmity. And it was those who made these poultices who made a lot of money. Woolworkers and vendors of remnants of cloth who found themselves in possession of cloths [after the death of the entrepreneur for whom they were working] sold it to whoever asked for it. When the mortality ended, those who found themselves with cloth of any kind or with raw materials for making cloth were enriched. But many [who actually owned cloths being processed by workers] found it to be moth-eaten, ruined or lost by the weavers. Large quantities of raw and processed wool were lost throughout the city and countryside.

This pestilence began in March, as was said, and ended in September 1348. And people began to return to look after their houses and possessions. And there were so many houses full of goods without a master that it was stupefying. Then those who would inherit these goods began to appear. And such it was that those who had nothing found themselves rich with what did not seem to be theirs and they were unseemly because of it. Women and men began to dress ostentatiously.

How Many of the Dead Died Because of the Mortality of the Year of Christ 1348?

Now it was ordered by the bishop and the Lords [of the city government] that they should formally inquire as to how many died in Florence. When it was seen at the beginning of October that no more persons were dying of the pestilence, they found that among males, females, children and adults, 96,000 died between March and October.

4. a shaved head, signifying membership in a religious order

The Role of Education in the Italian Renaissance

Paul F. Grendler

Paul F. Grendler is emeritus professor of history at the University of Toronto. He has written numerous articles on education during the Renaissance. In this article, he discusses the establishment and spread of humanism throughout Italy.

Education was seen as essential, for the people of the Renaissance regarded an educated populace as key to the growth and continued prosperity of the time. Each city and community desired quality education for its youth. Thus new schools were established and new teachers hired. These schools and teachers brought with them the humanist curriculum, which was then disseminated throughout the land, from the cities to the small towns.

Guarino [Guarini][1] and Vittorino [da Feltre][2] founded schools that trained the sons of the ruling class and future humanists. Convinced of the importance of an education based on the orators, poets, and historians, graduates of the schools of Guarino and Vittorino spread the knowledge of the *studia humanitatis*.[3] When these "old boys" reached positions of authority, they chose other pupils of the famous pedagogues,[4] classmates of lower social rank who had become teachers, to instruct their sons. Guarino and Vittorino helped by recommending their former students for teaching posts. In the way that influence works, humanistically trained masters gained teaching positions and implemented the new curriculum. Humanistic education became established in the 1430s, 1440s, and 1450s, especially in towns within the orbit of Guarino and Vittorino. The *studia humanitatis* soon spread

1. architect, poet, writer, and teacher   2. teacher and early humanist   3. curriculum of humanist studies   4. teachers

Paul F. Grendler, *Schooling in Renaissance Italy: Literacy and Learning, 1300–1600*. Baltimore: Johns Hopkins University Press, 1989. Copyright © 1989 by The Johns Hopkins University Press. All rights reserved. Reproduced with permission.

throughout northern and north-central Italy.

Numerous fifteenth-century humanists held elementary and secondary school teaching posts. The most ambitious and gifted men went on to become university professors, chancery secretaries, advisers to princes, and curial officials in Rome. Those who published little or lacked the good fortune to win the favor of the powerful remained in the elementary and secondary schools and solidified the triumph of the *studia humanitatis.*

The careers of students of [Gaparino] Barzizza,[5] Guarino, and Vittorino who became teachers illustrate the process. Martino Rizzoni, born circa 1404 in Verona, probably came from the middle ranks of society. He and his brother attended Guarino's school in Verona until their father died in 1424. Because Rizzoni had to earn a living, Guarino found him a post as tutor to a noble family in Venice. When Rizzoni complained that his noble pupils had little interest in studying and that the family treated him like a servant, Guarino encouraged him to persevere. He also persuaded Rizzoni's employer to raise the tutor's salary. Guarino continued to watch over Rizzoni's career, and Rizzoni performed minor scholarly tasks for his mentor. By 1432 Rizzoni had returned to Verona (Guarino having left); there he married and taught as an independent master for the rest of his life. His rising tax payments suggest that his school prospered. He also joined the scholarly circle around Ermolao Barbaro (probably a classmate in Guarino's school), who served as bishop of Verona from 1453 to 1481. Like other humanistic schoolmasters, Rizzoni wrote and delivered a number of nuptial orations and a grammatical work (now lost). He died in 1488.

Ognibene Bonisoli (Omnibonus Leonicenus) also helped spread the *studia humanitatis* through his teaching and writing. Born about 1412 in the small town of Lonigo about fifteen miles south of Vicenza and twenty-five miles west of Padua, Ognibene moved to Mantua as a child. There he studied with Vittorino da Feltre [a humanist educator] in the Casa Giocosa, possibly as an indigent pupil supported by the master, from about 1423 to about 1433. His schoolmate Ludovico Gonzaga remained Ognibene's friend long after becoming ruler of Mantua. After completing his

5. humanist teacher

schooling, Ognibene went to the Council of Basel,[6] and then to Vicenza, where he ran an independent school and married in or about 1436. He served Ludovico Gonzaga between 1436 and 1438 and taught independently in Treviso in 1440. Ognibene won a communal mastership at the relatively young age of about 29 when the Commune[7] of Treviso appointed him in January 1441 "to teach grammar and read rhetoric and whichever authors the students require" for five years at a salary of fifty ducats[8] per annum. The mention of rhetoric plus his background and scholarly activity confirm that Ognibene taught the *studia humanitatis.*

Ognibene accepted a communal mastership at Vicenza in 1443. In the next few years he declined offers to join the Venetian chancery and to become the tutor of Galeazzo Maria Sforza, future ruler of Milan (from 1466 to 1476). But when in 1449 Ludovico Gonzaga asked him to come to Mantua to tutor his eldest son and heir, Federico (d. 1484), and to assume leadership of the Casa Giocosa, Ognibene accepted. He remained in Mantua for four years, teaching the historian and humanist Bartolomeo Sacchi (il Platina, 1421–81), among others. Ognibene returned to his post as communal master of Vicenza in 1453 and remained there until his death in 1474. He won the affection of his students for his benevolence and pedagogical skill. . . .

New Teachers Spread Humanism

Ognibene's career typified the way humanism spread. He acquired mastery of his subject and met the political and economic elite of northern Italy in Vittorino's school. He then taught for four years as a court tutor, two to five as an independent master, and almost thirty as communal master. The civic leaders of Treviso and Vicenza hired him to teach; Gonzaga and Sforza princes wanted him as tutor. Ognibene did not forsake local schools for the court, chancery, or university, despite his considerable scholarly accomplishments. Nevertheless, through his teaching, scholarship, and contacts with the powerful, he aided the spread of the humanistic curriculum.

6. a meeting held to decide whether a council or the pope should govern the church   7. civic group formed to govern education for a town or area   8. gold coins that were the common currency of Venice during the Renaissance

A strong interest in the humanities for vocational purposes also aided the growth of the *studia humanitatis*. Over the course of the century, princes and governments, especially the most important in the peninsula, came to want their secretaries and other civil servants to be trained in the humanities. The Venetian Republic founded the Scuola di San Marco[9] in 1446 because La Serenissima[10] wanted humanistically trained secretaries. Rome offers another good example. After a few humanists such as Leonardo Bruni[11] and Poggio Bracciolini[12] found positions in the Roman curia[13] in the first decade of the fifteenth century, many others followed. Applicants with humanistic training had a clear edge in securing employment there from the pontificate of Nicholas V (1447–55) onward.

Thus, a humanistic education helped individuals climb the social ladder. The expanding Roman curia and other chanceries wanted more and more secretaries, abbreviators, and other officials who were well grounded in classical Latin and could write the new humanistic scripts. The posts carried good salaries in their own right and might lead to higher preferment, if the humanist also possessed diplomatic skills and political support. At the very least, a curial or secretarial post offered a secure living and improvement in the family's fortunes.

Such employment and opportunities and the example set by the governments of Florence, Rome, and Venice encouraged parents and communal councils to hire humanistic masters. Parents living far from the metropolitan centers also wanted their sons to have the humanistic training that made advancement possible. One suspects that few youths trained in *ars dictaminis* [the art of dictation] and unfamiliar with Cicero's epistles found chancery positions after 1450. Individuals did not need to have law degrees—although such degrees helped—to secure chancery positions, but thorough training in the *studia humanitatis* beginning in elementary school was a necessity.

As communal councils and parents hired humanistic schoolmasters, the *condotte* (contracts between employer and teacher) reflected the change in curriculum. The *condotte* used new ter-

9. the school of St. Mark   10. literally, "the most serene one," a nickname of Venice
11. a prominent humanist and teacher   12. humanist and historian   13. councils that assist the pope

minology to describe the curriculum and listed the teachers who gave effect to it. Masters were expected to teach the Latin orators, poets, and historians, or grammar, rhetoric, and poetry, plus Greek at times. Eventually the *condotte* specified which ancient authors and books must be taught. The terminology of medieval learning—*auctores*,[14] *ars dictaminis*, speculative grammar, *Eva columba*,[15] *Doctrinale*,[16] Boethius,[17] and so on—disappeared. Not being able to sit in their classrooms of long ago, we will never be certain that these teachers taught differently from their medieval predecessors. But a change in terminology indicated a commitment to the new curriculum. And if the new teachers were followers of Guarino and Vittorino, we can be sure that they taught the *studia humanitatis.*

Independent Schools Replace State and Church Schools

The lack of a strong ecclesiastical or state presence in pre-university education facilitated the switch to the new humanistic curriculum. Some bishops would have resisted the reading of more pagan authors had they exercised jurisdiction over communal and independent schools. In like manner, church schools, had they been numerous, might have been a formidable force for scholastic inertia. Instead, only a few clergymen (Giovanni Dominici[18] was one) opposed the reading of pagan authors as morally corrupting. Humanists answered that the ancient poets led readers to virtue through their stories of adultery and vice, and humanists carried public opinion. Since the church as an institution had very few schools and possessed no influence over communal and independent schools, it took no position. The same might be said for princes and republics, who only interested themselves in the few schools and teachers they supported. The lack of overall church and state control over schools allowed individual masters, parents, and city councils to make changes freely and quickly.

The change from medieval to Renaissance schooling can be seen in the extant teacher *condotte* of towns with ongoing com-

14. authors   15. literally "Dove of Eve"   16. doctrinal or instruction book   17. Roman philosopher, poet, and politician (480–525)   18. cardinal, statesman, and writer

munal schools. In 1376 the Commune of Spoleto (in Umbria) hired a master to teach "correct speech, speculative grammar, logic, and strict rhetoric," a typical late medieval curriculum. Spoleto continued to hire masters to teach grammar or *in gramaticalibus et poesi* in the early fifteenth century (1427). In 1432, a change occurred: the commune hired Pietro da Tolentino to teach grammar, poetry, and oratory (*pro scolis in gramaticalibus, poesi quoque et oratoria facultate in civitate gerendis*). In the absence of additional information we cannot be certain that an unknown teacher in a small town far distant from the humanistic centers of the Veneto or Florence inaugurated a humanistic curriculum at this early date. Nevertheless, the appointment notice signalled the beginning of change.

In 1371 Lucca [Italian city west of Florence] appointed a certain Antonio da Volterra to teach. The commune described his scholarly accomplishments: he has a doctorate in grammar and logic from Bologna, is an excellent "authorist" (*auctoristam optimum*), and is expert in philosophy. The combination of grammar, logic, *auctores*, and philosophy indicated a medieval curriculum.

In 1453 the Commune of Lucca wished to join the humanistic movement by offering a communal mastership to Giovanni Pietro d'Avenza, also called Gian Pietro da Lucca. Born in 1404 in Avenza, a tiny hamlet about twenty-five miles north of Lucca, Gian Pietro studied with Francesco Filelfo[19] for a short time in Florence, with Vittorino in Mantua, and with Guarino in Ferrara. He then taught school, possibly in Brescia, certainly in Verona and Venice. His scholarship included a grammar for school use, orations in which he strongly argued for the *studia humanitatis* as the key to cultural and civic formation, and extensive study of the works of Caesar and Livy. In 1450 he won the important appointment of master at the Scuola di San Marco, making him the second master to teach there. After an interval of illness in which another master substituted for him, Gian Pietro began at the Scuola di San Marco in 1451 teaching liberal studies (*ad legendum studia liberalia*).

Now, in 1453, the Luccans offered Gian Pietro the opportunity to return home. They offered him one hundred ducats (the same

19. humanist and scholar

salary he earned in Venice), plus permission to collect supplementary fees, to come to Lucca to teach "oratorical arts, poetry, and letters" ("in magistrum artis oratoriae, poesis et literarum"). Gian Pietro turned them down. The persistent Luccans renewed the offer in 1456, describing the appointment now as "rhetoric and oratorical art, poetry, and Greek and Latin letters" ("rhetoricam et artem oratoriam, poesim et licteras [sic] grecas atque latinas"). Gian Pietro accepted the offer, but he died in 1457, before he could have had much influence. Nevertheless, Lucca had joined its schools to the humanistic movement.

Humanist Influence Spans Italy

The Latin schools of other northern Italian towns also became humanistic by the middle of the fifteenth century. In 1446 Foligno appointed a communal master to teach "the rules of grammar, poets, historians, and books appropriate to the ability of the pupils" ("in legendo regulas gramaticales, poetas, historicos et libros convenientes secundum qualitatem auditorum"). In 1444 or 1449 the Commune of Treviso in the Venetian Dominion hired Filippo da Reggio[20] to teach grammar to boys and youths in the city of Treviso and to lecture on poetry and rhetoric to all who wish to attend." Moreover, the commune required Filippo "on feast days to lecture publicly on the art of oratory and such authors as his audience desire." In 1459 the Commune of Recanati for the first time described the duties of the communal master as "teaching grammar, rhetoric, and poetry" ("legere grammaticam, rhetoricam et poesim"). And in Modena, also in 1459, a teacher bought a house with the money that he had earned "from lecturing and teaching in schools grammar, the poets. rhetoric, and humanistic authors" ("ex exercitio legendi in scolis et docendi gramaticam, poetas, rhetoricam et humanitatis auctores").

Foligno, Treviso, and Recanati were not important towns by any definition in the fifteenth century or later. Yet, by the 1450s, they had humanistic communal masters. If such small and obscure towns had adopted the *studia humanitatis* by the 1450s, it is very likely that the majority, possibly a large majority, of northern and north-central Italian towns taught the humanistic cur-

20. teacher of rhetoric and the classics at the University of Pavia

riculum in their communal schools by the middle of the century. Communal schools had a significance greater than their numbers, because they embodied the educational preference of the town's leaders. Independent teachers could not have been far behind communal masters. The humanists had won.

The humanistic curriculum also moved south, although at a slower pace. Aldo Manuzio[21] (Aldus Manutius) recalled his early Latin education in the preface to his Latin grammar of 1501, addressed to teachers. Do not force children to memorize anything except the best authors, Aldo admonished. Of course they must learn inflections by heart, but do not force children to memorize the grammar book. I had to do this as a child, and I forgot everything in a hurry. In the time that students struggle to learn such things as grammar exercises, they could more easily and with greater profit memorize something of Cicero and Vergil. I regret that I could not do this as a child, but had to memorize a stupid work of verses of Alexander on grammar (the *Doctrinale* of Alexander de Villedieu).

Manuzio first saw light of day circa 1450, perhaps slightly earlier, in Bassiano, a tiny provincial hill town about fifty miles south of Rome. That Bassiano lacked a humanistic instructor in the late 1450s or early 1460s is not surprising. Aldo probably received no humanistic training until he moved to Rome (at an unknown date). There he studied with Gaspare da Verona[22] (c. 1400–1474) and Domizio Calderini[23] (1446–78) either at the University of Rome or in an elementary or secondary school.

But some provincial towns south of Rome boasted humanistic masters by the early 1470s. Had Aldo been born a few years later in nearby Velletri, twenty-five miles closer to Rome than Bassiano, he could have studied with an excellent humanistic teacher. By 1473 Antonio Mancinelli (1452–1505), a well-known humanistic pedagogue and author of Latin grammar textbooks, had opened a humanistic school in Velletri. Aldo was a little unlucky in his birthplace.

By the end of the fifteenth century, probably nearly all Latin schools in Italy were humanistic and commonly called "schools

---

21. classics scholar and printer   22. classics scholar and rhetorician   23. classics scholar and writer

of oratory, poetry, and grammar" ("scole in arte oratoria, poesi et gramatice"). Detailed curriculum prescriptions made the humanistic direction even clearer. For example, the Commune of Lucca in 1499 ordered its communal teachers to teach daily "a grammatical author, an historian, an orator or a book of epistles, a poet, and the rudiments of Greek" ("uno autore grammatico, uno historico, uno oratore overo uno libro di epistole, uno poeta et li erotimati greci"). Lucca renewed these instructions in 1524, 1546, and 1574, in identical or very similar words.

A few remnants of medieval schooling lingered. In 1498 the Commune of Pistoia instructed its communal master to teach grammar, rhetoric, *arte oratoria*, poetry, and Greek, but also "something or part or all of speculative grammar," if the pupils so wished. In the following year the commune ordered the master to teach daily the *Doctrinale* of Alexander de Villedieu, in addition to the standard Cicero and Vergil. Moreover, almost all humanistic schools retained *Donatus*[24] and the *Disticha Catonis*[25] for teaching beginning Latin grammar and reading.

These were small exceptions. Italian pedagogues had effected a curriculum revolution, one of the few in the history of Western education, in the relatively short time of about fifty years—1400 to 1450. They solidified their triumph by 1500. Boethius, *Graecismus, Facetus, Theodulus*,[26] and the rest of the curriculum authors gave way to Cicero, Terence, and Caesar. The *studia humanitatis* replaced *ars distaminis*. The *auctorista* disappeared; the humanist took his place.

24. refers to the Latin grammar text by Aelius Donatus   25. short moral sayings by Dionysius Cato   26. ancient writers taught in medieval curricula

A Country School in Tuscany

Arie S. Zmora

In Renaissance Italy, education was seen as the gateway to a better life and a better community. This belief was not limited to the cities and cultural centers. Many small towns developed sophisticated educational systems as well. Towns formed "communes" to oversee the schools. These communes went to great lengths to hire quality teachers and to provide their youth every opportunity to thrive and develop themselves.

Students from all walks of life were encouraged to attend these schools, and many went on to attend the universities as well. In fact, many small towns sent a higher percentage of students to universities than did the schools of the larger cities of the day. In the following article, Arie S. Zmora, former professor of history at St. Cloud State University, details just how important education was in the small towns of Italy.

Florence has long been enshrined in our collective memory as the cultural capital of Renaissance civilization. Surprisingly, the secondary cities, small towns, and hamlets of Tuscany (Arezzo, Borgo a Boiano, Lucca, Pietra Santa, Pisa, Pistoia, Prato, Volterra) throughout the sixteenth century and beyond had significantly larger numbers of university graduates per capita in the Studio Pisano, the flagship of the Tuscan university system, than did metropolitan Florence. The graduation records for the period 1543–99 reveal that while Florence claimed only five graduates per thousand inhabitants for that period, the secondary towns of Tuscany claimed a substantially larger number, and Pistoia surpassed them all by far with twenty-seven graduates per thousand inhabitants.

This accomplishment is especially intriguing because Renaissance contemporaries associated Pistoia with clan feuds, law-

Arie S. Zmora, "Schooling in Renaissance Pistoia: Community and Civic Humanism in Small-Town Tuscany," *Sixteenth Century Journal*, vol. 34, Fall 2003. Copyright © 2003 by Sixteenth Century Journal Publishers, Inc., Kirksville, MO 63501-0828 USA. All rights reserved. Reproduced by permission.

lessness, and violence. The pistol was named after the commune of Pistoia where it was first manufactured, further dramatizing the fact that Pistoians of the late Renaissance have long been associated with a culture of violence rather than with the pursuit of learning.

The achievements of Pistoian students at the university level were a direct result of the high quality of schooling they received prior to attending the university. This discussion examines the characteristics of schooling in small communes and assesses the advantages that students in these towns, particularly Pistoia, had in comparison to their peers from the large city. In particular, the activities of a charitable educational foundation, the Pia Casa di Sapienza, whose main function was to grant stipends to poor but talented students for university studies, is discussed and analyzed.

Renaissance scholars note that educators and municipal authorities were determined to teach children in accordance with their social status and family occupation. For example, sons of laborers or offspring of craftsmen were limited to studying the rudiments of mathematics and reading, and the type of schooling that communes provided was generally based on the social background of the students. The commune of Pistoia, however, sought to make schooling a shared experience accessible to a wider body of the municipality's youth from disparate backgrounds within the community. . . .

Successful Schools Lead to Successful Communities

Renaissance communities benefited immensely from a highly educated citizenry that shared a strong commitment to public service as political leaders of their respective communes. The connections among charity, education, and active citizenship were forcefully articulated by Pistoians. Members of the commune fully understood and emphasized the crucial role that education and schooling played in overcoming political chaos and sustaining viable community life and its municipal institutions. In this context, civic humanism underscores the collective efforts made by Pistoians to provide qualitatively good schooling to broad segments of the population, in order to ensure a broadly educated elite who, in turn, would be actively engaged in ruling the commune and safeguarding its independent and democratic nature.

With its population declining due to the flight of learned elite and the fierce factional strife between the Panciatichi and the Cancellieri clans at the end of the fifteenth century, the commune of Pistoia deliberately tried to reverse this trend by granting stipends to promising students. Their hope was that these students would return as accomplished professionals and assume leadership positions in the commune. Indeed, the success of the educational system in Pistoia reflects on the ways that Pistoians imbibed the spirit of civic humanism, effectively inculcating its principles throughout their educational system. Cardinal Forteguerri, a native son of Pistoia and a senior member of successive papal administrations of the quattrocento,[1] captured the magnitude of the crisis Pistoia faced in that period and lucidly articulated the solutions for the commune's problems. When bequeathing his patrimony to the commune, the cardinal drew the road map for the commune's salvation, invoking in his will the tenets of civic humanism: "keep in mind, that this city was driven to extreme poverty because it lacked learned citizens"; however, these circumstances could be radically improved since "citizens due to the study of letters and virtue, beyond any other means can rise and grow"; therefore, "an [educated] student would be eager to repay his country with faculties that God had bestowed upon him." The poor and the needy should not be discriminated against, argued the cardinal. Rather, they ought to receive the same opportunities as privileged, rich citizens, because human faculties are conferred by God, and cannot be pursued by "paternal help or riches.". . .

The municipality of Pistoia hired teachers skilled in particular areas of expertise at the grammar school level, including a teacher of writing (*maestro di scrivere*) and a teacher of arithmetic (*maestro di abaco*). These teachers taught grammar, reading and writing, and the rudiments of accounting. The minutes of the city council of Pistoia indicate an awareness of the importance of teaching these subjects as early as 1353. Members of the municipality justified the hiring of a teacher of arithmetic on the grounds that "merchants and artisans could not work profitably or as well

1. Italian Renaissance term for the fifteenth century

without the knowledge of *abaco*." This reasoning reflected the mercantile nature of Pistoia as well as a pragmatic attitude towards education that emphasized the contribution of schooling to the prosperity of the town as a whole, since artisans and merchants constituted the backbone of Pistoia's economy. Teachers of the elementary school level in Pistoia were hired on a contractual basis, through a *condotta*[2] that had to be renewed annually. The commune monitored the performance of elementary level teachers as closely as that of higher level instructors. From the 1560s, teachers were scrutinized regularly by a committee of "two citizens," usually individuals with doctoral degrees who were considered best qualified to evaluate the teachers' work. . . .

Ensuring a Quality Education

The proceedings of the city council meetings reveal details about the electoral process for teachers, including the general requirements and pedagogical qualifications of *maestri principali*,[3] and the curriculum that they were expected to teach. For instance, the minutes of the commune from 1469 describe the desirable *maestro principale* as "honest and learnt . . . who should teach grammar, read authors in verse and in prose." These instructions are more specific in the proceedings of 1511, enumerating a program of studies which followed the spirit of humanist pedagogical philosophy. The *maestro principale* was expected to "read authors, poets, orators, and historians." In addition, he was asked to devise a curriculum for slower learners as opposed to his more competent students: "Lessons should vary in accordance with the age and the intelligence of students." Whereas the less talented students were expected to memorize the rules of the written oration, their brighter counterparts were taught the creative aspects of oratory. Hence, they practiced and consequently enhanced their rhetorical skills by writing letters and orations.

A search for a *maestro principale* conducted in 1557 reveals additional details regarding the academic standards demanded of Pistoian students and the extent of the responsibilities of the *maestri principali* of the commune. Students "were expected to speak Latin in school" and to write epistles daily. The school

2. contract   3. headmasters

schedule was rigorous, beginning "at sunrise" and ending at two o'clock in the afternoon. Classes resumed in the evening, after the prayers of the Ave Maria were concluded, and continued until ten o'clock in the evening, always under the auspices of the *maestro principale*. . . .

In addition to their involvement in the administrative and disciplinary aspects of schooling, the *Sapienza*'s officials were also expected to monitor the academic and pedagogical performance of the commune's teachers. The municipal bylaws instructed the officials and custodians of the *Sapienza* to make sure that the teachers, namely the *maestri principali*, were actually teaching the topics for which they were hired. These rules suggest tight scrutiny of the teachers' and students' activities. Hence, the officials were asked to make sure that the *maestro principale* taught Latin and Greek "with all his energy and in a fearsome manner." These instructions were issued to prevent students from playing games during school time or occupying themselves in other "vain and dishonest activities" so that they "will study in a way which is fit for the pursuit of virtue."

Preparation for University

The crown of the educational system in Pistoia was the *collegio* of the *Sapienza*, which offered preuniversity schooling based on the program of studies at the *studio* of Pisa. The *collegio* was located at the *Sapienza*'s headquarters. It provided two years of preuniversity schooling in canon and civil law, rhetoric, and philosophy. The teaching positions in civil and canon law were entrusted to two doctors who were elected annually in accordance with the same electoral procedures used to elect the *Sapienza*'s students. With few exceptions, the elected doctors were *Sapienza* alumni who received an annual salary of 200 lire[4] each, which was slightly lower than a doctoral stipend of 30 ducats,[5] was comparable to the salary of a laborer in the construction industry of late-sixteenth-century Florence, and was sufficient to feed a family of four.

The fact that the *Sapienza* granted its alumni an opportunity

4. common currency of Italy   5. a gold coin that was the common currency of Venice during the Renaissance

to gain practical experience as lecturers further emphasized the personal responsibility and care that the foundation extended to its former students. The doctors were lecturers who, according to the bylaws, "read" in their prospective fields of expertise every morning "when the bells [of the duomo] rang." Every night, starting at 9:00 P.M., the students were taught rhetoric by listening to readings from Quintilian's *Institutions*[6] that were conducted by another doctor hired for that purpose. In these lessons students were expected to exercise "in writing" the different formulae of letters designed for a wide array of municipal issues, state affairs or ecclesiastical topics. The *Sapienza's* curriculum in rhetoric reflected the choices that the *collegio* offered in what Paul Grendler[7] terms "primary rhetoric" and "secondary rhetoric." The first form trained potential candidates in the oral traditions of delivering speeches for the more lucrative but scarce positions of envoys or ambassadors. The second, which emphasized the written aspects of rhetoric, prepared students for less prestigious yet more accessible positions in administrative offices in Pistoia, Florence, or the Roman Curia.[8] During these nocturnal hours, a doctor read texts in philosophy and logic. For their services, the teachers of rhetoric and philosophy earned an annual salary of 150 lire, a sum that was 25 percent less than the earnings of the law lecturers.

Establishing Public Libraries

Pistoia further demonstrated its sensitivity to the educational needs of its students by establishing a public library in the commune in the late 1400s. The renowned Pistoian humanist Sozomino donated his precious collection of classical manuscripts to the commune of Pistoia in his will. Sozomino, who was the son of a cobbler, rose to the height of Pistoian society. In the best traditions of civic humanism, he stipulated that the donation of his books to the commune was given on condition "that the commune will establish a public library where these books will be always available freely to everyone who wishes to study." Gio-

6. a book on rhetoric and education, often used as a textbook, written by early Roman rhetorician Quintilian   7. emeritus professor of history at the University of Toronto   8. the various ministries and organizations within the Catholic Church that assist the pope in carrying out the mission of the church

vanni di Bisticci, the Florentine humanist and renowned book-seller who organized the building of the Medici library, specifically underscored the importance of Sozomino's initiative in his lives of the most illustrious humanists of his time. The inventory of that collection, commissioned by the commune and carried out in 1460, includes some 150 manuscripts. These include virtually a whole spectrum of classical writing and historical works (Herodotus, Thucydides, Plutarch, Polibius, Livius, Salust, Suetonius, Tacitus, Flavius Josephus), classical literature (Homer, Virgil), philosophy (Plato, Aristotle), and rhetoric (Cicero, Quintilian), as well as the Renaissance humanist literature of Dante, Petrarch, Bruni, and Leon Battista Alberti.

This donation was intended to benefit and provide educational opportunities to the least fortunate members of Pistoian society at a time when books were increasingly associated with the social elite. In honoring the last wish of Sozomino, the city council of the commune decided in November 1458 to establish the library in the Palace of the Priori, in the halls of the *Abondanzza*, "which was the proper and honorable place." The significance of that decision can be surmised from the fact that "the first public library in modern times" had been established in the convent of San Marco in Florence only fourteen years earlier. Reading and possessing books was increasingly viewed by Tuscans as a symbol of social respectability and civility, and a mandatory element of the etiquette appropriate for a gentleman and member of the social elite.

When Niccolò Niccolini, a Florentine humanist, saw the sons of Pazzi aimlessly roaming the streets of Florence he perceived their behavior to be an embarrassment to their family name and pleaded with their father to let them read books instead. In his much acclaimed treatise on the family, *I Libri Della Famiglia*, Alberti urged his patrician contemporaries and their young offspring "to carry more often a book instead of a sword." Alberti emphasized the importance of books and libraries as necessary elements (*necessita vitali*) for the proper comportment of members of the social elite, comparable in importance to food, clothing, and horses. In a period when the printing press was in its infancy, offering unlimited and nondiscriminatory access to manuscripts was a radical concept, especially where access to culture was increasingly associated with the social elite. From the sixteenth century on, readers experienced difficulties in gaining access to books. The notion of a public library was novel to the early modern period, and when they were opened they operated in a rather erratic manner. A recent overview of libraries concluded that "in public libraries access was, as a rule, restricted to a privileged group." Robert Darnton,[9] for example, has illustrated how students in Leiden [in Holland] stood up to read books that were chained to shelves from shoulder-level counters. In contrast to these restrictions, Pistoia's approach of providing access to all was rooted in the liberal Renaissance tradition in Italy, following the example set by prestigious libraries such as the Vatican and the Ambrosian. . . .

Opportunities for Students

Once students of modest means graduated from the communal equivalent of high school they had the opportunity to pursue higher education. The bylaws of the *Sapienza* encouraged talented students from poor backgrounds to apply for financial assistance for their higher education. The provisions of the *Sapienza* were translated from Latin to the *volgare*[10] by explicit orders in the will of the deceased Cardinal Forteguerri. His intent was to reach a large audience of eligible youth who, due to the language barrier, might otherwise not have known about the stipends offered by the *Sapienza*. To guarantee maximum access to the benefits found in the *Sapienza*'s charter, the bylaws instructed that the charter of the foundation be written in clear calligraphy and in bold letters. These bylaws were housed in the offices of the *Sapienza*, and access to them for review by the interested public was unlimited. Twice a year these provisions were read aloud by officers of the *Sapienza* in the ceremonies conducted in the duomo of the commune during the induction of new students. This oral presentation provided an additional venue for dissemination of information regarding the educational opportunities offered by the *Sapienza*. There are at least five different copies in *volgare* of the *Sapienza*'s charter found in the Pistoian archives, a fact which testifies to the conscientious

9. professor of history at Princeton University   10. common, everyday language

effort made by the *Sapienza*'s officials to reach a wide audience, in accordance with the spirit of the *Sapienza*'s founding father Cardinal Forteguerri's will. Referring to the original objective of the foundation, the stipulations of the *Sapienza*'s bylaws set specific guidelines for choosing candidates for scholarships to pursue the *laurea* [bachelor's degree] in a university. The potential recipients of stipends were expected to be "at least eighteen years old, not rich," with a strong academic record and motivation to study. More specifically, the suitable candidate was expected to be "a good grammatician, an able (person) who was eager to study, as far as human fragility permits, theology, civic and canon law or medicine."

The *Sapienza*'s rules also mandated that a student be allowed to choose "freely," according to his interest, his own field of study. The only restriction was in regard to the study of medicine, where only one stipend was awarded. An amendment to the bylaws in the 1560s provided an additional stipend for the study of medicine, explaining, "it has been considered that this number is adequate to the needs of our community." The candidate had to be a citizen or a resident of the commune or its countryside for at least ten years. In view of the nepotistic traditions in Pistoia, these bylaws emphasized that only one person per family was eligible to be awarded a stipend of the *Sapienza* for up to the six years needed to attain the doctoral degree. An amendment to the *Sapienza*'s bylaws in 1530 accommodated the commune's social realities by allowing two members of the same family to be eligible concurrently to hold the *Sapienza*'s stipends. In order to ensure academic success, prospective students were expected to graduate from the *collegio* of the *Sapienza* or from any other studio that offered a similar academic curriculum. These regulations became more stringent during the early seventeenth century when the city council determined that only those candidates who graduated from the *collegio* of the *Sapienza* would be able to renew stipends. . . .

The educational experience in Pistoia illuminates the egalitarian quality of education that the commune offered for its sons, which stands in striking contrast to the prevailing views of schooling during the Renaissance. This egalitarianism was not absolute, since, in spite of its charter, almost half of stipend recipients in the *Sapienza* were members of the commune elite. The *Sapienza*, however, managed to avoid to a considerable extent the pitfalls of the patronage system.

The motives for these policies are varied. First, the commune allocated public resources to guarantee qualitative schooling for all of the town's students, which reflects on the commitment of Pistoians to the tenets of civic humanism. Second, there may have been a heightened sense of religious piety and sensitivity to social justice that distinguished the commune of Pistoia from other communities in Italy. Third, broad access to schooling might reflect a divided oligarchy that sought allies among the "little people," who in turn won some dividends for their offspring in education as a pay-off for their allegiances. In all likelihood the opportunities offered to Pistoian students were the result of a successful, though quite ironic, merger between pragmatic considerations of power and the community's long-standing commitment to serving the cause of the public good. . . .

The school system in Pistoia provided its sons with exceptional preuniversity preparation allowing them to excel later in the university. Yet the Pistoians' educational experience was by no means an isolated success story. On the contrary, the large numbers of university graduates, who were native sons of small towns of Tuscany, reflects a broader European pattern. Studies of public schooling in France and Spain of the early modern period reveal that these countries' provincial towns provided better education for students than their peers gained in the schools of larger cities. It may well be that the small towns in contrast to large metropolitan centers shared a different, perhaps more dynamic pattern of social interaction. The size of cities, distribution of wealth among the citizens, social hierarchies, and informal nature of social rapport in small towns all seem to be important factors, suggesting further lines of inquiry in regard to the surprising advantages that small towns offer in schooling when compared to large cities.

On a final note, scholars of the medieval and the early modern period often compare the experience of the metropolitan centers vis-à-vis life in the small villages. That comparison emphasizes the dramatic contrast between life in a rural, sparsely populated, loosely organized village versus a densely populated, socially segregated, highly regulated, walled city. Such a comparison overlooks small towns as sites of another type of experience. Recent historiography is filling that void by studying small towns and this case study of schooling in Pistoia demonstrates how useful such studies can be in providing a fuller understanding of the urban experience of the early modern period.

Art and Culture

CHAPTER

3

Gloucester Library
P.O. Box 2380
Gloucester, VA 23061

Chapter Preface

When discussing the Renaissance, the most talked about aspect of the time is often the great developments in art and culture. The explosion of art, sculpture, and architecture is yet to be rivaled, as the period produced many of the best-known names in each field.

The names are many, the works of art copious, the buildings breathtaking. Many of the most famous pieces of art in the world come from the Renaissance: Michelangelo's statue of David, symbolizing the power and might of the relatively small city of Florence; Leonardo da Vinci's enigmatic *Mona Lisa*, the most reproduced painting of all time; Brunelleschi's Duomo, which baffles architects to this day. These works are part of the consciousness of the art historian and the casual observer alike.

One force that encouraged art during the Renaissance was the concept of patronage, in which wealthy families, individuals, or the church sponsored works of art, either for public or private display. Under the patronage of the great families of Florence, Venice, and Rome, Renaissance artists were given the time and resources necessary to create their fantastic masterpieces.

Though noble in spirit, patronage was also driven by the great amount of competition between families within a city, as well as between cities, towns, and regions. Each desired to prove their wealth and taste by commissioning the greatest buildings, sculpture, and paintings. The art, both public and private, became a measuring stick of one's power and status.

In the public sector and the private sphere, art played an important role in everyday life. Buildings needed to be beautiful and awe-inspiring, courtyards needed to be decorated with sculpture, houses needed to have great paintings. Everywhere one looked in Renaissance Italy, he or she could find the touches of a great master. Art was tightly integrated into every aspect of life. Thus the artists of the Renaissance were given many opportunities to showcase their skills.

Perhaps the most easily recognized part of its legacy, the art and culture of the Renaissance are one of its greatest contributions. The names are world renowned, their impact immeasurable.

Interplay of Art and Culture

George Holmes

The fact that art played a large role in Renaissance culture is well documented. From the sketches of Leonardo to the sculptures of Michelangelo, the world is replete with examples of incredible pieces from the period. In this selection, noted Oxford historian George Holmes describes the setting and interactions that led to such a rich development of the arts.

One of the main factors in the explosion of art during the Italian Renaissance was the financial prosperity of the time. A great emphasis was placed on the visual arts as many sought to express the ideals of humanism through their work. The literature of the period was a venue for disseminating the new ideals as well.

The art of the Renaissance was such a vital part of the culture of the day that it developed at an incredible rate, much faster than in the rest of Europe, and became a symbol of the intellectual and financial prosperity of the time.

The surge of cultural achievement which is evident in some parts of Italy around the year 1300 had as its most important cause the commercial success of some of the great cities, which produced a more urban civilization, different from the society which had existed earlier in Italy or contemporaneously in the rest of Europe. But there were other important contributory factors. If we think of the cities of Florence, Siena, and Pisa—all of which were in Tuscany—their intellectual evolution was affected by the memory of ancient Rome, now dead but still spiritually alive in writings of Vergil and Cicero, and in the vast monuments scattered about the city itself. An equally powerful influence was exerted by modern Rome, the city of the popes and the capital of the western Church. The civilization of Renaissance Italy had to live, easily or uneasily, with the Christian Church.

George Holmes, "Renaissance Culture," *The Oxford History of Italy*, edited by George Holmes. Oxford, UK: Oxford University Press, 1997. Copyright © 1997 by Oxford University Press. All rights reserved. Reproduced by permission.

The greatest and most original of the new breed of creators was Dante Alighieri (1265–1321), the writer of the *Divine Comedy*. Serious poetic creation in the Italian tongue, unlike the medieval tongues of northern Europe, scarcely stretched back before 1250. Dante, first schooled by other gentlemen-poets of the Tuscan towns, wrote a long and complex poem which has never ceased to dominate the Italian mind as Homer did the mind of Greece. The *Divine Comedy* was composed by Dante in the years of exile between his expulsion from Florence in 1302 and his death in 1321. The three sections of Hell, Purgatory, and Paradise are entirely symmetrical in form and also linked by the fictional figures of Dante himself, who visits all three levels of the universe, and the lady Beatrice, an idol of love in the old poetic tradition, transformed into a redeemed and all-knowing inhabitant of Heaven. But the subject-matter of the poem covers a very wide variety of topics which provide a conspectus of Dante's own life and of many of the pressing concerns of his Italy. A large part is played by the political problems of strife in cities, dominated by great families and factions, and of the political claims of the popes, who wished to be theocratic emperors in Italy. Dante was probably also much influenced by the teaching of the Spiritual wing of the Franciscan Order which gave him, at least for a time, an apocalyptic expectation of the future history of the Church and the Holy Roman Empire. *Paradiso*, the last of the three *cantiche* [sections], expressed his acceptance of the philosophical theology of the greatest of medieval Italian philosophers, St Thomas Aquinas (d. 1274), who had attempted an elaborate accommodation to each other of the rationalist philosophy of Aristotle and the revelation offered by the Bible. Aquinas had done most of his philosophizing at Paris. Italy had several important universities, including the great law school at Bologna and the university of Padua, close to Venice, famous for its devotion to Aristotle's scientific and medical works. Dante, however, was very much the product of Florence and expressed in the fullest way the new culture of the City, partially free of ecclesiastical and academic domination in its thought—Florence as yet had no university—and therefore a receptacle fitted for the spirit of the new humanism, which was to play a dominant role in Italian culture for the next three hundred years.

The culture of Renaissance Italy was to give exceptional prominence to the visual arts. Humanism was to be expressed as much by painting and sculpture as by literature. The resurgence of the visual arts began, it might be argued, as much in Rome, and in Assisi, under Roman influence, as in Florence. Siena and Pisa were also important because it was there that Niccolò and Giovanni Pisano, father and son, inaugurated the imitation of Roman sculptural remains which very quickly developed into a new kind of figural naturalism. Giovanni Pisano's figures at Sant' Andrea, Pistoia, and at the cathedrals of Pisa and Siena reached a high level of sophistication in the presentation of the human form. It was the case at several stages in the history of Renaissance art that sculpture *preceded* painting. One is inclined indeed to apply this opinion not only to Giovanni Pisano in the late thirteenth century but also to Donatello and Ghiberti in the fifteenth and to some extent to Michelangelo in the sixteenth. However this may be, much of the later Renaissance seems already present in Giovanni's pliant and vital human figures and the painters of the next generation were to some extent imitating the stone figures of Giovanni Pisano and Arnolfo di Cambio rather than nature.

Thirteenth-century painting was inseparable from the Franciscan Order, first and most successful of the new mendicant orders which flooded Italy with their friars and transformed its cities with their huge convents. The Franciscans promoted the visual presentation of the events of the life of St Francis (d. 1226) and the great double basilica built at Assisi, where the order originated, contained several series of frescoes, painted in the late thirteenth and early fourteenth centuries, which gave a powerful impulse to that type of art. Most notable was the great series of the life of St Francis in the upper basilica, providing a visual interpretation of the account written by St Bonaventure, which became the accepted record of stories such as that of St Francis preaching to the birds.

The names of most of the painters at Assisi are unknown, those of the main series of St Francis's life totally unknown. It is generally thought that papal patronage and influence led to much of the fresco work being done by Roman painters and that thus the reconsideration of the ancient Roman traditions, which seems to have been active but whose productions in Rome itself have been largely destroyed by the rebuilding of the sixteenth and seventeenth centuries, was given a prominent place at Assisi, where it inspired artists from further north. However that may be, the great painter who was most obviously inspired by Assisi, and may have worked there, was the Florentine Giotto (d. 1337). Giotto may also have met Dante in exile at Padua; if that is so the two main founders of the Renaissance aesthetic tradition were linked. Giotto was in Padua to cover with frescoes the interiors of the Arena Chapel, his most important surviving work. The chapel was paid for by a rich man, acting on an impulse which must have owed something to the model of Assisi. Giotto produced a series of scenes illustrating the life of Christ preceded by the lives of the Virgin Mary and her apocryphal mother Anne. The series of scenes is remarkable for its dramatic quality: the episodes lead into each other to present a tragic battle between good and evil. But perhaps more important was Giotto's attempt to give each scene a spatial reality. This was the beginning of the movement which was eventually to lead to Brunelleschi's invention of mathematical perspective and Leonardo's further scientific projects. Giotto's space was by these standards primitive and his perspective rough and ready and based largely on the relationship of a few figures to a simple architectural space, often the interior of a single room. Nevertheless the leap to an art in which the figures were clearly placed in space, not simply related notionally to it and to other figures, was sudden. Also the figures were given a new discernible weight, most noticeable perhaps in the altarpiece of the enthroned Virgin and Child, the *Ognissanti Madonna*, now in the Uffizi at Florence, which made a striking advance in naturalism over the countless other panel-paintings of thirteenth-century Italy. Traditionally such altarpieces, made to stand behind altars or to be carried in processions, required by the fervent popular religion which was associated especially with the Franciscans and Dominicans and many other orders, had served a symbolic rather than a realistic purpose. That psychology was now changing.

Sienese Painting and Petrarch

Giotto's greatest contemporary was the Sienese painter Duccio (d. 1318). Siena, though not as large as Florence, was also a notable commercial centre and, in the period before the Black Death of 1348, was able to command a visual culture of similar splendour. The Sienese, who had built their cathedral in the thirteenth century, were hoping in the early fourteenth to enlarge it into the greatest structure of that kind in the world and were prevented from doing this only by the physical instability of the site and the demographic disaster of 1348. Duccio was the artist chosen to paint the *Maestà*, a grand celebration of the Virgin, the traditional protectress of Siena, and her Son, to stand behind the altar of the cathedral. It was finished in 1311, a series of painted wooden panels, fixed together, which gave a detailed account of the life of Christ, particularly of the events leading up to the Passion and beyond. Duccio's concerns were different from those of Giotto. His interest in space and figural weight was much weaker. But he was extraordinarily successful in presenting a vivid story, in which, for example, the command of elegant figures and the grace of the structural pattern were stronger than Giotto's. The *Maestá* (1309–11) was produced almost at the same time as the Arena Chapel (c. 1305–10). They were both ambitious works covering the life of Christ by painters whose origins were only about 50 miles apart. It is interesting—and a testimony to Italian inventiveness—that it should have been possible for two such strong, but divergent, traditions to arise in such close proximity to each other.

In the first half of the fourteenth century Siena continued to produce inventive painters. After Duccio the development of the representation of space proceeded further than at Florence, particularly in the work of Ambrogio Lorenzetti (d. 1348). His *Presentation* (1342), now in the Uffizi at Florence, shows the biblical scene taking place in an elaborate church, whose side aisles and chancel can be seen receding into the background of the picture. This carries Giotto's spatial naturalism a good deal further and in fact was not to be improved on before the next century. A few years earlier Lorenzetti had painted a series of frescoes illustrating the themes of good and bad government in the Palazzo Pubblico at Siena, which were a striking illustration of the political ideals of the republican city. Some of them are allegorical but two scenes, which are fairly well preserved, show the *Well-Governed Town* and the *Well-Governed Countryside*. The latter is in one sense a presentation of the whole *contado* of Siena [territories controlled by Siena], stretching to its seaport on the coast, a view of over 40 miles, of course unrealistic. But, taken as a painting of countryside, it is a daring attempt to present a realistic space of fields and hills, not defined by walls, which again was not improved on or rivalled in the fourteenth century.

Another major Sienese painter, Simone Martini (d. 1344), ended his career at the papal court in France. There the Papacy had resided since 1305 and remained until 1377. This 'Babylonish Captivity', as some regarded it, deprived Italy and Rome of the papal court and its artistic and intellectual patronage for a long time. There Simone Martini met another Italian exile, the writer Petrarch (1304–74), apparently drew Petrarch's beloved Laura, and was admired by the writer. Here then is another meeting of artist and writer, succeeding the—-possibly legendary—meeting of Dante and Giotto, and foreshadowing the well-documented and very important intercourse of humanists and artists to come later. Petrarch has often been regarded as the founder of humanism, but, although he spent much of his time outside Italy, he belongs to the tradition of lay education and learning, which existed before him and which was one of the important national peculiarities of Italian society throughout the Renaissance period. The notary, who wrote formal documents in Italian and Latin, was the Italian equivalent of the modern solicitor, and because of the importance of Latin to him, he often took an interest in the classical writings of Cicero. Petrarch was the son of a notary and partly trained as a lawyer at Bologna, to follow in his father's footsteps. Instead he gave it up to become a professional literary man.

Although he sprang out of an earlier tradition, Petrarch was a man with quite exceptional innovative creativity. It is difficult to think of any other literary artist so fecund in the invention of literary genres. He is best remembered nowadays for the Petrarchan sonnet and his Italian poetry was a powerful influence throughout the Renaissance period. But he was also the inventor of the scientific study of Latin texts and of the dialogue, wrote lives of the heroes of ancient Rome, attempted a Latin poem in imitation of Vergil, and castigated the scholastic philosophy which was prevalent in the universities. Petrarch earned his living by writing and in 1341 was crowned with the laurel on the Capitol at Rome, by order of King Robert of Naples. He was the first modern man of letters.

To grasp the nature of Petrarch's cast of mind it is probably best to look at his *Secretum*, mostly composed about 1347. This is a dialogue, the prototype of hundreds of dialogues composed later in the Renaissance, a discussion between two characters—Augustine, based on St Augustine, and Francis, based on Petrarch's name Francesco Petrarca—who represent the two tendencies struggling within Petrarch's mind. Augustine presents the austere Christian doctrine that this life is merely a preparation for death, Francis presents Petrarch's personal attachment to a life of love and glory arising from his skill as a poet. The debate is unresolved. Petrarch was both, on the one side a lover and poet, on the other a being disturbed by the fear that the monastic life was the true purpose of humanity. In the *Secretum* he gave a picture of the underlying dilemma which was to run unsolved through the whole of Renaissance culture: how to reconcile the worldly purposes based on a literary humanism derived from pagan Rome with the Christian self-denial and devotion to heaven preached by the religious orders. Both were strongly rooted movements in the Italian world and, though many made attempts at reconciliation, notably, as we shall see, Marsilio Ficino and Michelangelo, the problem was insoluble.

Petrarch's greatest literary contemporary was a very different person, Giovanni Boccaccio (1313–75), also a man of letters and precursor of more modern writers, but this time rooted in the Florentine city world, which he occasionally served as an envoy. Boccaccio is best remembered for his *Decameron*, the long series of stories imagined as told by Florentine gentlefolk in flight from the plague of 1348. The *Decameron* is a literary adaptation of city story-telling, witty, fantastic, often anticlerical or obscene, and it is written in Italian. In historical perspective it shows one way in which the Italian imagination might have developed. With Boccaccio's stories, Petrarch's poems, and the *Divine Comedy* literature in Italian had very rapidly, within a hundred years, reached a high level of success, which made it at the very least comparable with, perhaps superior to, the achievements of medieval French and German. Why not continue on this path? Boccaccio himself was an example of the tensions which turned the Italian mind in another direction for he was also fascinated by classical literature. One of his last compositions was the *Genealogy of the Pagan Gods*, in Latin, which told the classical stories in a manner which was acceptable to the Christian and was in fact to have a long celebrity as a repository of classical legend. As it turned out the next century, the fifteenth, was to see much classical humanism and little first-class writing in Italian, in one sense an impoverishment, in another an enrichment of the Italian genius.

The Humanist Revolution

The explosion of humanist scholarship and writing which took place at the beginning of the fifteenth century marked a turning-away both from city gossip and from Christianity. One of the conditions of its success was the collapse of papal authority during the Great Schism, 1378–1415, which followed the return of Pope Gregory XI from Avignon to Rome and split the College of Cardinals, leading to support for two rival popes for a whole generation. In these circumstances of papal weakness devotion to classical literature grew unchecked at Florence, promoted by a group led by the chancellor, or chief civil servant, of the city, Coluccio Salutati. After 1415, when the Papacy was reunited at Rome and papal prestige and wealth revived, the papal court became once again an important centre of patronage for Italians, which it had ceased to be in 1305, and the link between humanists at Florence and Rome was strong and important. 'Humanism' is an imprecise word which can only be taken to mean a devotion to the supreme cultural value of classical literature and thought. Though the definition is vague the instinct it represents was of very great importance to Italians for the next two centuries. . . .

In spite of its origins in its enjoyment of the pagan classics humanism did not come seriously into conflict with ecclesiastical authority, and popes, notably Nicholas V (1447–55), happily patronized the translation of Thucydides and other Greek writers into Latin with as much equanimity as they planned the rebuilding of Rome to revive ancient glories. Even the writings of Lorenzo Valla (1407–57), a Roman by origin who used his linguistic skill to criticize the Latin Vulgate translation of the Bible and the translation of Greek philosophers' words by several scholastics, did not upset the friendly alliance of classics and Christianity. The most influential of the Roman humanists was Leon Battista Alberti (1404–72) who wrote the only important humanist text of this period in Italian, *On the Family*, a work of political and social thought which was again indifferent to the old obsession with Church-State relations, and instead took as its subject the family within the context of the secular city. Alberti, however, was still more original than this. He began the crucial movement of alliance between humanism and the visual arts which was to fructify in the glorious century and a half of Italian art which started in the early fifteenth century. Alberti's book *On Painting* (1436) was a work by a rich and learned humanist inspired by the artistic craftsmen—so they were commonly regarded—of contemporary Florence. It did two things. First it established a new set of aims for painting: to reproduce scenes naturalistically, using perspective and giving figures an appearance which was true to their emotions; to use the colours of nature, avoiding decorative gold and silver, to tell a story. Secondly it proclaimed the artist to be a man of culture like the literary humanist. Florentines had adulated Giotto among their great men but now the artist was to be part of the company of cultivated gentlemen, a quite different role from that of the artisan with a physical skill. Alberti also wrote a book about architecture in which he advocated planned cities and a classical style. Again it was both in tune with the intellectual ethos of the time and an innovative book, carrying ideas unexpectedly further. As Bruni transformed the Italian mind, Alberti did more than anyone else to change the face of Italy.

Humanism and Art

Alberti's inspiration was the revolution in the visual arts which took place at Florence. The key figures were Filippo Brunelleschi (1377–1446), architect and sculptor, and Donatello the sculptor. Again, as in 1300, sculpture advanced a little ahead of painting. The new movement would have been impossible without the assistance of literary humanists, who advised the use of classical models and helped to patronize the new work. But it also required the skill of the craftsman. Great skill was required to devise the dome which Brunelleschi managed to place above the crossing of the Gothic cathedral of Florence, in imitation of the Pantheon at Rome and the Byzantine domes of Constantinople; great skill also was needed for the complex casting of the bronze of Donatello's *Judith and Holofernes*. Florence was a rich society with many brilliant artisans and much interest in palatial decoration. The basis of the artistic evolution was also, however, a fairly sudden determination, under humanist influence, to turn to classical models.

Brunelleschi's architecture in the loggia of the Innocenti orphanage made the decisive turn from the pointed arches of Gothic, normal in Italy as elsewhere throughout Europe, to the round arches of Roman architecture. Thus it became possible to develop an architecture which was based on the circle and the square, very different from the assumptions of the Gothic past. While a medieval church had been essentially a lengthy procession towards the altar, the trend was now essentially towards the concentric church, enclosed in cupolas and rounded arches. Brunelleschi moved towards this in his Florentine churches of San Lorenzo and Santo Spirito. Later came Alberti's architecture based more intellectually on the study of actual Roman remains, which found one of its main practical expressions at Sant' Andrea, Mantua, designed by him, where the huge and heavy arches foreshadowed the later development of churches. In the next generation came Donato Bramante (d. 1514), a Lombard whose most famous work was done at Rome, who went the whole way to the completely concentric church at San Pietro in Montorio, on a hill above the Vatican. Bramante was eventually to design the new St Peter's for Julius II, and this too was intended to be a concentric church in the form of a Greek cross, without the huge nave which was added by later masters. Thus the triumph of the Roman-Mediterranean spirit in architecture was complete.

It provided a setting for sculpture, again in imitation of classical remains. Brunelleschi had a friend and collaborator in Donatello (1386–1466) who was avid in his acceptance of classical inspiration and profound in his mastery of dramatic emotion expressed in stone and bronze, perhaps the greatest of all European sculptors. Donatello produced a long series of works, stretching from the first to the seventh decades of the century, which transformed sculpture through their examination of a wide variety of human figures and forms, from the confident beauty and innocence of the *Annunciation* in Santa Croce at Florence to the sinuous attractiveness of the *Bronze David* (Bargello, Florence) and the experience of suffering in the Christ of the late *Resurrection* relief (San Lorenzo, Florence). Donatello was fully awake to the demands of new spatial ideas of perspective and to the adoption of motifs taken over from ancient art but he added to these an exceptional grasp of humanity, which would be difficult to parallel. . . .

There were schools of painting which grew up under the aegis of local tyrants anxious to enjoy modern culture and to add splendour to their capitals. The political fragmentation of Italy meant that centres of culture grew up not only in Florence, Venice, and Rome but also in petty states ruled by tyrants with taste: the Visconti and Sforza of Milan, the Gonzaga of Mantua, the Montefeltro of Urbino, to mention only the notable families of patrons. The lords of Urbino, for example, patronized Piero della Francesca (d. 1492), a painter who was not a member of the Florentine school, though he had learned from it, an enthusiast for perspective with the mathematical interest to write treatises about it. Both Piero's great series of frescoes of the *Legend of the Holly Tree* at San Francesco in Arezzo, telling the story from the time of Adam to the rediscovery of the cross by Helena and after, and his *Flagellation* at Urbino with its elaborate and delicate perspective drawing, show that it was possible for provincial art to reach the highest levels and that the existence, for political reasons, of a very large number of centres of patronage made possible a remarkably widespread variety of artistic achievement.

It was at this period that Italy clearly outstripped the rest of Europe in the luxuriousness of its artistic life. In the mid-century Alberti's Tempio Malatestiano at Rimini—another work paid for by a provincial despot—was a completely classical piece of architecture. The chapel of the Cardinal of Portugal at San Miniato, Florence, was produced in the 1460s by the joint efforts of architect, sculptor, and painter with extraordinarily delicate luxuriance. These and other artistic works set standards which would be followed by the rest of Europe, starting at least a century behind.

The Development of a Renaissance Artist

Giorgio Vasari

Giorgio Vasari was an architect, writer, and painter in Italy during the sixteenth century. His collection of biographies of the great artists of the Renaissance, *Lives of the Artists*, is an extremely important work. Much of the information about Renaissance artists that historians rely on today comes from this work. It is an impressive collection of facts, some of which have been updated by scholars, but most of which have stood the test of time. Just as important are his critical judgments, which show significant insight and are, for the most part, unbiased.

In the following excerpt, Vasari traces the development of Leonardo da Vinci, from overachieving yet distracted student, to apprentice artist, to great master and inventor. He reveals Leonardo to be a practical joker, a constant inventor, and a determined painter. Leonardo's development as an artist was such that he was soon better than his teacher, who quit drawing as a result.

Marvellous and divine, indeed, was Lionardo the son of Ser Piero da Vinci. In erudition and letters he would have distinguished himself, if he had not been variable and unstable. For he set himself to learn many things, and when he had begun them gave them up. In arithmetic, during the few months that he applied himself to it, he made such progress that he often perplexed his master by the doubts and difficulties that he propounded. He gave some time to the study of music, and learnt to play on the lute, improvising songs most divinely. But though he applied himself to such various subjects, he never laid aside drawing and modelling in relief, to which his fancy inclined him more than to anything else; which Ser Piero perceiving, he took some of his drawings one day and carried them to Andrea del Verrocchio,[1] with whom he was in close friendship, and prayed

1. Florentine sculptor and painter

Giorgio Vasari, *Lives of Seventy of the Most Eminent Painters, Sculptors, and Architects*, edited by E.H. and E.W. Blashfield and A.A. Hopkins. New York: C. Scribner's Sons, 1896.

him to say whether he thought, if Lionardo gave himself up to drawing, he would succeed. Andrea was astounded at the great beginning Lionardo had made, and urged Ser Piero to make him apply himself to it. So he arranged with Lionardo that he was to go to Andrea's workshop, which Lionardo did very willingly, and set himself to practice every art in which design has a part. For he had such a marvellous mind that, besides being a good geometrician, he worked at modelling (making while a boy some laughing women's heads, and some heads of children which seem to have come from a master's hand), and also made many designs for architecture; and he was the first, while he was still quite young, to discuss the question of making a channel for the river Arno from Pisa to Florence. He made models of mills and presses, and machines to be worked by water, and designs for tunnelling through mountains, and levers and cranes for raising great weights, so that it seemed that his brain never ceased inventing; and many of these drawings are still scattered about. Among them was one drawn for some of the citizens when governing Florence, to show how it would be possible to lift up the church of S. Giovanni, and put steps under it without throwing it down; and he supported his scheme with such strong reasons as made it appear possible, though as soon as he was gone every one felt in his mind how impossible it really was.

He delighted much in horses and also in all other animals, and often when passing by the places where they sold birds he would take them out of their cages, and paying the price that was asked for them, would let them fly away into the air, restoring to them their lost liberty.

Sharpening His Skills

While, as we have said, he was studying art under Andrea del Verrocchio, the latter was painting a picture of S. John baptizing Christ. Lionardo worked upon an angel who was holding the clothes, and although he was so young, he managed it so well that Lionardo's angel was better than Andrea's figures, which was the cause of Andrea's never touching colours again, being angry that a boy should know more than he.

There is a story that Ser Piero, being at his country house, was asked by one of the country people to get a round piece of wood, which he had cut from a figtree, painted for him in Florence, which he very willingly undertook to do, as the man was skilled in catching birds and fishing, and was very serviceable to Ser Piero in these sports. So having it brought to Florence without telling Lionardo where it came from, he asked him to paint something upon it. Lionardo, finding it crooked and rough, straightened it by means of fire, and gave it to a turner that it might be made smooth and even. Then having prepared it for painting, he began to think what he could paint upon it that would frighten every one that saw it, having the effect of the head of Medusa. So he brought for this purpose to his room, which no one entered but himself, lizards, grasshoppers, serpents, butterflies, locusts, bats, and other strange animals of the kind, and from them all he produced a great animal so horrible and fearful that it seemed to poison the air with its fiery breath. This he represented coming out of some dark broken rocks, with venom issuing from its open jaws, fire from its eyes, and smoke from its nostrils, a monstrous and horrible thing indeed. And he suffered much in doing it, for the smell in the room of these dead animals was very bad, though Lionardo did not feel it from the love he bore to art. When the work was finished, Lionardo told his father that he could send for it when he liked. And Ser Piero going one morning to the room for it, when he knocked at the door, Lionardo opened it, and telling him to wait a little, turned back into the room, placed the picture in the light, and arranged the window so as to darken the room a little, and then brought him in to see it. Ser Piero at the first sight started back, not perceiving that the creature that he saw was painted, and was turning to go, when Lionardo stopped him saying, "The work answers the purpose for which it was made. Take it then, for that was the effect I wanted to produce." The thing seemed marvellous to Ser Piero, and he praised greatly Lionardo's whimsical idea. And secretly buying from a merchant another circular piece of wood, painted with a heart pierced with a dart, he gave it to the countryman, who remained grateful to him as long as he lived. But Lionardo's Ser Piero sold to some merchants in Florence for a hundred ducats,[2] and it soon came into the hands of the Duke of Milan, who bought it of them for three hundred ducats.

2. a gold coin that was the common currency of Venice during the Renaissance

Lionardo was so pleased whenever he saw a strange head or beard or hair of unusual appearance that he would follow such a person a whole day, and so learn him by heart, that when he reached home he could draw him as if he were present. There are many of these heads to be seen, both of men and women, such as the head of Americo Vespucci,[3] which is the head of an old man most beautifully drawn in chalk; and also of Scaramuccia, captain of the gipsies. When Giovan Galeazzo, Duke of Milan, was dead, and Lodovico Sforza became duke in the year 1494, Lionardo was brought to Milan to play the lute before him, in which he greatly delighted. Lionardo brought an instrument which he had made himself, a new and strange thing made mostly of silver, in the form of a horse's head, that the tube might be larger and the sound more sonorous, by which he surpassed all the other musicians who were assembled there. Besides, he was the best improvisatore of his time. The duke, hearing his marvellous discourse, became enamoured of his talents to an incredible degree, and prayed him to paint an altarpiece of the Nativity, which he sent to the emperor.

His Famous Works

He also painted in Milan for the friars of S. Domenic, at S. Maria delle Grazie, a Last Supper; a thing most beautiful and marvellous. He gave to the heads of the apostles great majesty and beauty, but left that of Christ imperfect, not thinking it possible to give that celestial divinity which is required for the representation of Christ. The work, finished after this sort, has always been held by the Milanese in the greatest veneration, and by strangers also, because Lionardo imagined, and has succeeded in expressing, the desire that has entered the minds of the apostles to know who is betraying their Master. So in the face of each one may be seen love, fear, indignation, or grief at not being able to understand the meaning of Christ; and this excites no less astonishment than the obstinate hatred and treachery to be seen in Judas. Besides this, every lesser part of the work shows an incredible diligence; even in the tablecloth the weaver's work is imitated in a way that could not be better in the thing itself.

3. explorer who realized the Americas were separate from Asia

It is said that the prior of the place was very importunate in urging Lionardo to finish the work, it seeming strange to him to see Lionardo standing half a day lost in thought; and he would have liked him never to have put down his pencil, as if it were a work like digging the garden. And this not being enough, he complained to the duke, and was so hot about it that he was constrained to send for Lionardo and urge him to the work. Lionardo, knowing the prince to be acute and intelligent, was ready to discuss the matter with him, which he would not do with the prior. He reasoned about art, and showed him that men of genius may be working when they seem to be doing the least, working out inventions in their minds, and forming those perfect ideas which afterwards they express with their hands. He added that he still had two heads to do; that of Christ, which he would not seek for in the world, and which he could not hope that his imagination would be able to conceive of such beauty and celestial grace as was fit for the incarnate divinity. Besides this, that of Judas was wanting, which he was considering, not thinking himself capable of imagining a form to express the face of him who after receiving so many benefits had a soul so evil that he was resolved to betray his Lord and the creator of the world; but this second he was looking for, and if he could find no better there was always the head of this importunate and foolish prior. This moved the duke marvellously to laughter, and he said he was a thousand times right. So the poor prior, quite confused, left off urging him and left him alone, and Lionardo finished Judas's head, which is a true portrait of treachery and cruelty. But that of Christ, as we have said, he left imperfect. The excellence of this picture, both in composition and incomparable finish of execution, made the King of France desire to carry it into his kingdom, and he tried every way to find architects who could bring it safely, not considering the expense, so much he desired to have it. But as it was painted on the wall his Majesty could not have his will, and it [remained] with the Milanese refectory, and while he was working at Supper, he painted Lodovico [duke of Milan, 1494–1500] with his eldest son, Massimiliano, and on the other side the Duchess Beatrice with Francesco her other son, both afterwards Dukes of Milan. While he was employed upon this work he proposed to the duke that he should make a bronze equestrian statue of marvellous size to perpetuate the memory of the Duke (Francesco Sforza). He began it, but made the model of such a size that it could never be completed. There are some who say that Lionardo began it so large because he did not mean to finish it, as with many of his

Leonardo da Vinci's Mona Lisa *is among the most admired and influential paintings of the Renaissance.*

other things. But in truth his mind, being so surpassingly great, was often brought to a stand[still] because it was too adventuresome, and the cause of his leaving so many things imperfect was his search for excellence after excellence, and perfection after perfection. And those who saw the clay model that Lionardo made, said they had never seen anything more beautiful or more superb, and this was in existence until the French came to Milan with Louis, King of France, when they broke it to pieces. There was also a small model in wax, which is lost, which was considered perfect, and a book of the anatomy of the horse which he made in his studies. Afterwards with greater care he gave himself to the study of human anatomy, aided by, and in his turn aiding, that of Messer Marc Antonio della Torre, who was one of the first to shed light upon anatomy, which up to that time had been lost in the shades of ignorance. In this he was much helped by Lionardo, who made a book with drawings in red chalk, outlined with a pen, of the bones and muscles which he had dissected with his own hand. There are also some writings of Lionardo written backward with the left hand, treating of painting and methods of drawing and colouring.

In his time the King of France came to Milan, and Lionardo was entreated to make something strange for his reception, upon which he constructed a lion, which advanced some steps and then opened his breast and showed it full of lilies. Having returned to Florence, he found that the Servite monks had entrusted [Italian painter] Filippino with the work of painting an altarpiece; but when Filippino heard that Lionardo had said he should have liked such a piece of work, like the courteous man he was, he left off working at it, and the friars brought Lionardo to their convent that he might paint it, providing both for himself and his household. For a long time, however, he did nothing, but at last he made a cartoon[4] of our Lady with S. Anne and the infant Christ, which not only astonished all artists, but when it was finished, for two days his room was filled with men and women, young and old, going as to a solemn festival to see Lionardo's marvels.

This cartoon afterwards went to France. But he gave up the

4. a full-sized preliminary sketch

work for the friars, who recalled Filippino, but he was surprised by death before he could finish it.

Lionardo undertook to paint for Francesco del Giocondo[5] a portrait of Mona Lisa, his wife, but having spent four years upon it, left it unfinished. This work now belongs to King Francis of France, and whoever wishes to see how art can imitate nature may learn from this head. Mona Lisa being most beautiful, he used, while he was painting her, to have men to sing and play to her and buffoons to amuse her, to take away that look of melancholy which is so often seen in portraits; and in this of Lionardo's there is a peaceful smile more divine than human. By the excellence of the works of this most divine of artists his fame was grown so great that all who delighted in art, and in fact the whole city, desired to have some memorial of it. And the Gonfalonier[6] and the chief citizens agreed that, the Great Hall of the Council having been rebuilt, Lionardo should be charged to paint some great work there. Therefore, accepting the work, Lionardo began a cartoon representing the story of Nicolo Piccinino, captain of the Duke Filippo of Milan, in which he drew a group of cavalry fighting for a standard, representing vividly the rage and fury both of the men and the horses, two of which, with their forefeet entangled, are making war no less fiercely with their teeth than those who ride them. We cannot describe the variety of the soldiers' garments, with their crests and other ornaments, and the masterly power he showed in the forms of the horses, whose muscular strength and beauty of grace he knew better than any other man. It is said that for drawing this cartoon he erected an ingenious scaffolding that could be raised and lowered. And desiring to paint the wall in oil, he made a composition to cover the wall; but when he began to paint upon it, it proved so unsuccessful that he shortly abandoned it altogether.

There is a story that having gone to the bank for the sum which he was accustomed to receive from the Gonfalonier Piero Soderini every month, the cashier wanted to give him some packets of farthings,[7] but he refused to take them, saying, "I am no farthing painter." As some accused him of having cheated Soderini in not finishing the picture, there arose murmurs against him, upon

5. a wealthy merchant in Florence   6. chief magistrate   7. coins of little value

which Lionardo, by the help of his friends, collected the money and restored it to him, but Piero would not accept it.

When Leo was made Pope, Lionardo went to Rome with Duke Giuliano de' Medici, and knowing the Pope to be fond of philosophy, especially alchemy, he used to make little animals of a wax paste, which as he walked along he would fill with wind by blowing into them, and so make them fly in the air, until the wind being exhausted, they dropped to the ground. The vine-dresser of the Belvedere having found a very strange lizard, Lionardo made some wings of the scales of other lizards and fastened them on its back with a mixture of quicksilver, so that they trembled when it walked; and having made for it eyes, horns, and a beard, he tamed it and kept it in a box, but all his friends to whom he showed it used to run away from fear.

It is said that when the Pope entrusted him with some work for him he immediately began to distil oil for the varnish, upon which Pope Leo said, "Oh, this is a man to do nothing, for he thinks of the end before he begins his work."

There was great ill-feeling between him and Michael Angelo Buonarroti,[8] on which account Michael Angelo left Florence. But when Lionardo heard this, he set out and went into France, where the king, having already some of his works, was well affectioned towards him, and desired that he should colour his cartoon of S. Anne; but he, according to his custom, kept him waiting a long time. At last, having become old, he lay ill for many months, and seeing himself near death, he set himself to study the holy Christian religion, and though he could not stand, desired to leave his bed with the help of his friends and servants to receive the Holy Sacrament. Then the king, who used often and lovingly to visit him, came in, and he, raising himself respectfully to sit up in bed, spoke of his sickness, and how he had offended God and man by not working at his art as he ought. Then there came a paroxysm, a forerunner of death, and the king raised him and lifted his head to help him and lessen the pain, whereupon his spirit, knowing it could have no greater honour, passed away in the king's arms in the seventy-fifth year of his age.

The loss of Lionardo was mourned out of measure by all who

8. Michelangelo, sculptor and painter

had known him, for there was none who had done such honour to painting. The splendour of his great beauty could calm the saddest soul, and his words could move the most obdurate mind. His great strength could restrain the most violent fury, and he could bend an iron knocker or a horseshoe as if it were lead. He was liberal to his friends, rich and poor, if they had talent and worth; and indeed as Florence had the greatest of gifts in his birth, so she suffered an infinite loss in his death.

Uses of Art in Renaissance Italy

Peter Burke

Peter Burke, professor of history at the University of Cambridge, provides a look at the various uses of art during the Renaissance. Art was not simply to be viewed and enjoyed, though there was a place for that as well. Art was a powerful tool that was used to communicate in many arenas.

In religion, art was sacred, a symbol of higher things. It pointed to God and the saints. It helped remind people of the important stories and traditions of their faith. In the political realm, art was used to inspire people to civic duty, to denigrate a rival, or to highlight an achievement. However, it was also created for enjoyment, though even this purpose was twofold. Often, art seemingly made for the enjoyment of all was also intended to show a city's wealth or importance.

The idea of a 'work of art' is a modern one, although art galleries and museums encourage us to project it into the past. Even the idea of 'literature' is a modern one. This [selection], however, is concerned with the different uses, for contemporary owners, viewers or listeners, of paintings, statues, poems, plays and so on. They did not regard these objects in the same ways as we do. For one thing, paintings might be regarded as expendable. A Florentine patrician, Filippo Strozzi the younger, asked in his will of 1537 for a monument in the family chapel in Santa Maria Novella, which contained a fresco by Filippino Lippi.[1] 'Do not worry about the painting which is there now, which it is necessary to destroy', Strozzi ordered, 'since of its nature it is not very durable [*di sua natura non é molto durabile*].' If we want to understand what the art of the period meant to contemporaries, we have to look first at its uses.

1. Florentine painter (1457–1504)

Peter Burke, *The Italian Renaissance: Culture and Society in Italy*. Princeton, NJ: Princeton University Press, 1987. Copyright © 1986 by Peter Burke. First edition published in 1972 by Batsford, UK; Scribner, U.S. paperback edition published by Collins Fontanta in 1974. This revised edition first published in 1987 by Princeton University Press. All rights reserved. Reproduced by permission.

Religion and Magic

The most obvious use of paintings and statues in Renaissance Italy was religious. In a secular culture like ours, we may well have to remind ourselves that what we see as a 'work of art' was viewed by contemporaries primarily as a sacred image. The idea of a 'religious' use is not very precise, so it is probably helpful to distinguish magical, devotional and didactic functions, although these divisions blur into one another, while 'magic' does not have quite the same meaning for us as it did for a sixteenth-century theologian. It is more precise and so more useful to refer to the thaumaturgic and other miraculous powers attributed to particular images, as in the case of certain famous Byzantine icons. Some gonfalons or processional banners, for example those painted by Benedetto Bonfigli[2] in Perugia, seem to have been considered a defence against plague. The Madonna is shown protecting her people with her mantle against the arrows of the plague, and the inscription on one gonfalon begs her 'to ask and help thy son to take the fury away.' The popularity in the fifteenth and sixteenth centuries of images of St Sebastian, who was also associated with defence against plague, suggests that the thaumaturgic function was still an important one. When he was working in Italy in the 1420s and 1430s, the Netherlander Guillaume Dufay wrote two motets to St Sebastian as a defence against plague. Music was generally believed to have therapeutic power; stories were current about cures effected by playing to the patient.

A celebrated Italian example of another kind of miraculous power is the image of the Virgin Mary in the church of Impruneta, near Florence, which was carried in procession to produce rain in times of drought or to stop the rain when there was too much, as well as to solve the political problems of the Florentines. For example, the Florentine apothecary Luca Landucci records in his journal that in 1483 the image was brought to Florence 'for the sake of obtaining fine weather, as it had rained for more than a month. And it immediately became fine.'

Some Renaissance paintings appear to belong to a magical system outside the Christian framework. The frescos by [Italian

---

2. Italian painter from Perugia (1420–1496)

painter] Francesco del Cossa in the Palazzo Schifanoia at Ferrara are concerned with astrological themes, as Aby Warburg[3] pointed out, and they may well have been painted to ensure the good fortune of the duke. It has also been argued (following a suggestion of Warburg's) that Botticelli's[4] famous *Primavera* may have been a talisman, in other words an image made in order to draw down favourable 'influences' from the planet Venus. We know that the philosopher [Marsilio] Ficino made use of such images, just as he played 'martial' music to attract influences from Mars. . . . When Leonardo (as Vasari[5] tells us) painted the thousand-eyed Argus guarding the treasury of the duke of Milan, it is difficult to tell whether he simply intended to make an appropriate classical allusion or whether he was also attempting a piece of protective magic. It is similarly difficult to tell how serious Vasari is being when he works a variant of the Byzantine icon legends into his life of Raphael.[6] He tells us that a painting of Raphael's was on the way to Palermo when a storm arose and the ship was wrecked. The painting, however, 'remained unharmed . . . because even the fury of the winds and the waves of the sea had respect for the beauty of such a work'. In a similar way, we need at least to entertain the possibility that the images of traitors and rebels painted on the walls of public buildings in Florence and elsewhere were a form of magical destruction of fugitives who were beyond the reach of conventional punishment; the equivalent of piercing wax images of one's enemies.

Other images were made and bought in order to stimulate devotion. The term 'devotional pictures' (*quadri di devotione*) was current in this period, when images and religious fervour seem to have been more closely associated than usual, whether the images were crucifixes (recommended by leading preachers such as Bernardino of Siena[7] and [Girolamo] Savonarola[8]) or the new medium of the woodcut, or a new type of religious painting, small and intimate, suitable for a private house, not so much an icon as a narrative, which would act as a stimulus to meditation

3. German art historian (1866–1929)   4. Florentine painter and student of Filippino Lippi (1445–1510)   5. writer, painter, and architect who wrote a series of biographies about the great artists of the Renaissance   6. painter and architect from Urbino (1483–1520)   7. friar and itinerant preacher (1380–1444)   8. Dominican monk and reformer (1452–1498)

on the Bible or the lives of the saints.

A vivid illustration of the devotional uses of the image comes from Rome, from the fraternity of St John Beheaded (*San Giovanni Decollato*), which comforted condemned criminals in their last moments by means of *tavolette*, in other words small pictures of the martyrdom of saints which were employed, in the words of their recent historian, 'as a kind of visual narcotic to numb the fear and pain of the condemned criminal during his terrible journey to the scaffold.'

The increasing importance of devotional images seems to have been linked to the increasing lay initiatives in religious matters characteristic of the fourteenth and fifteenth centuries, from the foundation of religious fraternities to the singing of

Religious images, such as those in Titian's Madonna and Child with Saints, *were commonly used in Renaissance art.*

hymns or the reading of pious books at home. Surviving inventories of the houses of the wealthy reveal images of Our Lady in almost every room. In the castle of the Uzzano family, Florentine patricians, there were two paintings of the 'sudary' (Christ's face imprinted on Veronica's towel), and immediately before one of them a predella is listed, as if people commonly knelt before the sacred image.

As the fifteenth-century friar Giovanni Dominici put it, parents should keep sacred images in the house because of their moral effect on the children. The infant Jesus with St John would be good for boys, and also pictures of the Massacre of the Innocents, 'in order to make them afraid of arms and armed men'. Girls, on the other hand, should fix their gaze on Saints Agnes,[9] Cecilia,[10] Elizabeth,[11] Catherine,[12] and Ursula[13] (with her legendary 11,000 virgins) to give them 'a love of virginity, a desire for Christ, a hatred for sins, a contempt for vanities'. In a similar way, Florentine girls, whether young nuns or young brides, would be given images, or more exactly dolls, of the Christ-child to encourage identification with his mother. . . .

Another use of religious paintings was didactic. As pope Gregory the Great[14] had already pointed out in the sixth century, 'Paintings are placed in churches so that the illiterate can read on the walls what they cannot read in books.' A good deal of Christian doctrine was illustrated in Italian church frescos of the fourteenth centuries: the life of Christ, the relation between the Old and New Testaments, the Last Judgement and its consequences and so on. The religious plays of the period consider many of the same themes, so that each medium reinforced the message of the others and made it more intelligible.

A special case of the didactic is the presentation of controversial topics from a one-sided point of view, in other words, propaganda. Like rhetoric, painting was a means of persuasion. Paintings commissioned by Renaissance popes, for example, present arguments for the primacy of popes over general councils of the Church sometimes by drawing historical parallels. For pope

9. martyr who was killed for refusing to make sacrifices to pagan gods.   10. martyr who was arrested for burying other martyrs   11. daughter of the king of Hungary who built a hospital   12. counseled Pope Gregory XI and Urban VI   13. martyr who was killed along with her companions   14. pope from 590 to 604

Sixtus IV,[15] for example, Botticelli painted the *Punishment of Korah*, illustrating a scene from the Old Testament in which the earth opened and swallowed up Korah and his men after they had dared to challenge Moses and Aaron. An earlier fifteenth-century pope, Eugenius IV,[16] had made reference to Korah when condemning the Council of Basel.[17] In a similar manner, Raphael painted for pope Julius II,[18] who was in conflict with the Bentivoglio family of Bologna, the story of Heliodorus,[19] who tried to plunder the Temple of Jerusalem but was expelled by angels. Again, after the Reformation, paintings in Catholic churches in Italy and elsewhere tended to illustrate points of doctrine which the Protestants had challenged.

Following the Reformation, the Catholic Church became much more concerned to control literature and, to a lesser degree, painting. An Index of Prohibited Books was drawn up (and made official at the Council of Trent[20] in the 1560s), and Boccaccio's[21] *Decameron*, among other works of Italian literature, was first banned and then severely expurgated. Michelangelo's *Last Judgement* was discussed at the Council of Trent, which ordered the naked bodies to be covered by figleaves. An Index of Prohibited Images was considered, and [painter Paolo] Veronese was on one occasion summoned before the Inquisition of Venice to explain why he had included in a painting of the *Last Supper* what the inquisitors called 'buffoons, drunkards, Germans, dwarfs and similar vulgarities.'

Politics

The visual defence of the Papacy has introduced the subject of political propaganda, at least in the vague sense of images and texts glorifying or justifying a particular regime, if not in the more precise sense of recommending a particular policy. There are so many examples of glorification from this period that it is difficult to know where to begin, whether to look at republics or principalities, at large-scale works such as frescos or small-scale ones such as medals. Like the coins of ancient Rome, the medals of Renaissance Italy often carried political messages. Alfonso of Aragon,[22]

15. pope from 1471 to 1484   16. pope from 1431 to 1447   17. called by Pope Martin V in 1431   18. pope from 1503 to 1513.   19. Syrian statesman (ca. 175 B.C.)   20. called in 1545 to respond to the challenge of Protestantism   21. novelist (1313–1375)   22. conquered and ruled Naples from 1435 to 1458

for example, had his portrait medal by Pisanello[23] (1449) inscribed 'Victorious and a Peacemaker [*Triumphator et Pacificus*].' On his triumphal arch there was a similar inscription, 'Pious, Merciful, Unvanquished [*Pius, Clemens, Invictus*]'. The king, who had recently won Naples by force of arms, seems to be telling his new subjects that if they submit they will come to no harm, but that in a conflict he is bound to win. In Florence, at the end of the regime of the elder Cosimo de' Medici,[24] a medal was struck showing Florence, personified in the usual manner as a young woman, with the inscription 'Peace and Public Liberty [*Pax Libertasque Publica*]'. Under Lorenzo the Magnificent,[25] medals were struck to commemorate particular events, such as the defeat of the Pazzi conspiracy[26] or Lorenzo's successful return from Naples in 1480. The sculptor Gian Cristoforo Romano commemorated the peace arranged between Ferdinand of Aragon and Louis XII with a medal giving the credit to pope Julius II and describing him as 'the restorer of justice, peace and faith [*Iustitiae pacis fideique recuperator*]'. Mechanically reproducible as they were, and relatively cheap, medals were a good medium for spreading political messages and giving a regime a good image.

Statues displayed in public were another way of glorifying warriors, princes and republics. Donatello's[27] great equestrian statue at Padua honours a *condottiere*[28] in Venetian service, Erasmo da Narni, nicknamed 'Gattamelata', who died in 1443, and it was commissioned by the state. (By contrast, the monument to Bartolommeo Colleoni in Venice was effectively paid for by the *condottiere* himself.) A number of Florentine statues had a political meaning which is no longer immediately apparent. In their wars with greater powers (notably Milan), the Florentines came to identify with David defeating Goliath, with Judith cutting off the head of the Assyrian captain Holofernes,[29] or with St George[30] (leaving Milan the role of the dragon). Donatello's memorable renderings of all three figures are thus republican statements. When the Flo-

23. painter and draftsman (1395–1455)   24. ruler of Florence (1519–1574)   25. ruler of Florence (1449–1492)   26. plot against Lorenzo the Magnificent and his brother Giuliano de' Medici to attempt to wrest control of Florence from the Medici family   27. Florentine sculptor; one of the major innovators of the Renaissance (1386–1466)   28. mercenaries who battled for the powerful families of the Renaissance   29. story from the Apocrypha in which Judith kills the commander of the army arrayed against Israel   30. myth in which St George kills the dragon that was terrorizing a town

rentine Republic was restored in 1494, political symbols of this kind reappeared, notably Michelangelo's great *David*, which refers back to Donatello's *David*[31] and so by extension to the dangers which the Republic had successfully survived in the early fifteenth century. The statue thus 'demands a knowledge of contemporary political events before one can understand it as a work of art.'

Paintings, too, carried political meanings. In Venice, the Republic was glorified by the commissioning and display of official portraits of its doges,[32] and of scenes of Venetian victories in the Hall of the Great Council in the Doge's Palace. In Florence, when the Republic was restored in 1494, a Great Council was set up on the Venetian model, together with a hall in the Palazzo della Signoria as a meeting-place, complete with victory paintings on the walls, the battles of Anghiari and Cascina commissioned from Leonardo and Michelangelo. When the Medici returned in 1513, the paintings were destroyed. This destruction of works by major artists suggests that the political uses of art were taken extremely seriously by contemporaries; so does the employment of Vasari, Bronzino[33] and other painters by Cosimo de' Medici, grand duke of Tuscany, to redecorate the Palazzo Vecchio with frescos of the achievements of the regime and to paint official portraits of the grand-ducal family. What is more difficult to decide, at this distance in time, is whether certain paintings carried more precise messages; whether, for example, they recommended certain policies. One example which has attracted considerable attention is Masaccio's[34] great fresco of *The Tribute Money* in the Brancacci Chapel in Santa Maria del Carmine in Florence. The subject is an unusual one; it carries a clear moral, 'Render unto Caesar', and it was painted at a time, 1425, when proposals to introduce a new tax, the famous *catasto*,[35] were under discussion. Is it a pictorial defence of the tax? Or is its message one about papal primacy, like Botticelli's *Punishment of Korah*? . . .

Art for Pleasure

We arrive at last at what now seems the natural 'use' of the arts: to give pleasure. The playful side of the arts must not be forgot-

31. bronze statue of David standing over the head of Goliath   32. chief magistrates   33. Florentine painter (1503–1572)   34. Florentine painter (1401–1428)   35. a comprehensive taxation plan in Florence

ten, although it has not often been studied. The increasing importance of this function is one of the most significant changes in the period. By the mid–sixteenth century, the writer Lodovico Dolce went so far as to suggest that the purpose of painting was 'chiefly to give pleasure [*principalmente per dilettare*]'. The carnival song of the sculptors of Florence catches the new mood. It should be noticed, however, that as the song makes clear, pleasure (*diletto*) is taken in the statue as a contribution to interior decoration. We are still a long way from modern ideas of 'art for art's sake'. Even the Gonzagas,[36] who cared a good deal about painting, seem to have thought of it primarily in this way. Isabella[37] asked Giovanni Bellini[38] for a picture 'to decorate a study of ours [*per ornamento d'uno nostro studio*]', while her son Federico wrote to Titian[39] in 1537 telling him that the new rooms in the castle were finished, all that was lacking were the pictures 'made for these rooms [*fatte per tali lochi*]'. Sabba di Castiglione, a knight of the Order of Rhodes, gave some advice, which has become notorious, for the decoration of a nobleman's house with classical statues or, if these are not available, with works by Donatello or Michelangelo.

In architecture, we see the increasing importance of the pleasure house, the country villa, where, as the greatest designer of such houses, Palladio, put it, a man 'tired of the bustle of cities, will restore and console himself'. In literature too there was increasing emphasis (especially in prefaces) on pleasure—the author's, and more particularly the reader's—a shift which may well be related to the gradual commercialization of literature and art.

36. ruling family in Mantua   37. Isabella d'Este, marquesa of Mantua   38. founder of the Venetian school of painting (1430–1516)   39. Venetian artist (1588–1576)

Entertainment and Music

Jean Lucas-Dubreton

The people of the Renaissance enjoyed an active and varied social life. When the workday ended, many took to the streets, talking, arguing, and visiting the taverns of the city. Concerts occurred regularly, as the love of music permeated the culture. The musical landscape of the time was changing as quickly as the artistic, with new instruments being developed and new rhythms and melodies adapted. In this piece, French historian Jean Lucas-Dubreton colorfully discusses this vibrant culture.

Throughout Italy there were festivals, public games, and races, with colorful displays and wonderful settings. A city or town was often judged by the extravagance of its festivals. The theater was also a major part of Renaissance life, with new plays and productions that reflected the time and the people. Though they were an industrious people, with impressive economic and artistic production, the Italians of the Renaissance were also a people who enjoyed the entertainments and music of their day.

As soon as he had laid down his work, which was often late—as he was a great worker—the artisan, according to Varchi,[1] lived better than the merchant. He went from tavern to tavern, and then into the street or on to the public square, and enjoyed himself, observing the crowd or arguing endlessly. He might be seen at the Banchi [main street through Florence], unrestrained in his speech, prompt in retort, and not in the least disillusioned by political and other kinds of gossip which were the daily bread of his existence. The atmosphere was joyous, noisy and sometimes feverish; and people spoke with their hands:

'With the hands one summons or dismisses, one rejoices or sorrows, calls for noise or silence, for prayers or threats, for peace

---

1. poet and historian who wrote a history of Florence (1502–1565)

Jean Lucas-Dubreton, *Daily Life in Florence in the Time of the Medici*, translated by A. Lytton Sells. New York: Allen & Unwin, 1960. Copyright © 1960 by George Allen & Unwin Ltd. All rights reserved. Reproduced by permission.

or rioting; one affirms and denies, demonstrates and counts. The hands reason, argue and finally agree; they adapt themselves to each one of our intentions.' So writes Matteo Palmieri, a merchant who knew all about it.

Sometimes on summer nights the strains of a concert, or the human voice, might be heard. In the days of Lorenzo the Magnificent[2] it was a virtuoso named Luigi Pulci (different from the poet Gigi) who improvised; and so great was his talent that the young Michelangelo rushed to hear him as soon as he discovered his whereabouts.

Music Was Everywhere

Every Florentine loved music. It beguiled the fatigue of the workman toiling under the hot sun; it cheered the peasant girl who had risen before dawn to spin and weave; nature had taught music to the nurse to pacify the wailing infant. The study of music therefore was recommended. Its rapid measures made the body alert and 'trained it to adopt graceful attitudes'. It exercised and nurtured the mind, corrected the voice and rendered pronunciation soft, accented, grave or sonorous.

In the course of time the sway of music increased, instruments were improved and diversified; organ, harpsichord, violin, lute, lyre, 'cello, harp, horn, trombone—all shaped in forms elegant or bizarre. In 1480 a school of harmony grew up in the entourage of Lorenzo de' Medici and under the direction of Antonia Squarcialupi, a famous organist. It was a sort of academy, and included painters and sculptors who were also musicians (note by the way the part played by musicians in Italian painting). Here recitals would be given by a quartet of stringed instruments, *quattro viole da arco*. For song, one voice was preferred to a choir, because one voice could be better heard, enjoyed and judged.

At the beginning of the sixteenth century a revolution was initiated by Stefanello, who was organist at St Mark's in Venice. Music was now allied to drama, which it supported and developed. There was now not one orchestra but several, with different instruments, each orchestra being attached to an individual actor. Thus in Poliziano's *Orfeo*, the contrabass viols accompanied Or-

2. Lorenzo de' Medici, ruler of Florence (1449–1492)

pheus,[3] the treble viols Eurydice,[4] the trombones Pluto,[5] the flutes and bag-pipes the shepherds. Curiously enough, Charon, the ferryman of Hades, was accompanied by guitars. In the preludes and *ritornelli* all the instruments took part; the accompaniment was then a symphony, the musicians executing the same partitions as the actors were to sing, or had sung, on the stage.

To return to the open street, here complete liberty seemed to obtain, although the police-spies kept an eye on certain classes of men, such as former exiles who had been recalled in cases where their ability or their work was advantageous to the city. The carrying of arms and observation of the curfew were also supervised. Yet, on the whole, the Florentine had no feeling of being curbed or bridled, and he also enjoyed great freedom of mind in the midst of civic disturbances.

Many Entertainment Options

Street-scenes delighted him, and some of them are worth recording. Thus in April 1489, when the foundations were being laid for the Palazzo Strozzi, a small tradesman named Tribaldo de' Rossi arrived at the spot and threw into the trenches an old soldo,[6] bearing a 'commemorative' lily. He then called his little boy Guarnieri and his daughter Francesca. 'Tita, our servant,' he relates, 'had come to the shop for meat, as it was Thursday. She then went to fetch the children, and my wife Nannina sent them both dressed to me. I took them to see the foundations, and raised Guarnieri in my arms, so that he could look down into them. As he had a little bunch of Damascus roses, I made him throw them down and said: "You will remember this, won't you?" He replied "Yes." They were with Tita, and Guarnieri was exactly four years and two days old. Nannina had recently made him a new jacket of shot-silk, green and yellow. . . .'

The foundation of a palace for a great family was a public event in Florence. But Tribaldo and his fellow-tradesmen were never at a loss for diversion. They could visit the botanical garden at Careggi, the Medici villa, where many different kinds of trees were growing; and in Florence itself, near the Palazzo, the

---

3. the greatest musician and poet from Greek mythology   4. Eurydice was in love with Orpheus; he tried to retrieve her after she had been bitten by a serpent and sent to Hades.   5. Roman god of the Underworld   6. coin

serraglio or menagerie. Here there was a den of lions, who were held in special esteem as the lion was the emblem of Florentine independence. He figured on the city arms. To touch him was a crime. His sicknesses or his death were a presage of catastrophe; when on the other hand a lioness bore many cubs, this was a sign of prosperity. The lion-keeper, a bearded and hairy fellow, was held in fearful veneration.

In addition to lions, leopards, bears, wild boars and bulls played a part in public festivities, as for example at the reception of Pope Pius II, a Siennese, in 1453. That day, however, the lions were a disappointment, as they lay down and refused to attack the other animals. A ball was given in the Mercato Vecchio by way of consoling the public.

Stags and buffaloes were sometimes brought in, and the fête then took the form of a hunt. The apothecary Landucci describes one which took place in 1514 in the Piazza della Signoria. In the middle of the square a grove of verdure had been arranged, with a fountain, where the animals could rest and quench their thirst. Never had there been so many visitors and strangers. There were even cardinals in disguise, garbed in black, wearing swords and concealing their faces.

The joiners and contractors had paid up to forty florins for building platforms along the house fronts. In the open were shelters known as 'tortoises', under cover of which men goaded the animals with lances. Once again the lions remained torpid. One of them, after killing a dog, lost all interest in the proceedings. There were casualties, however, three men being killed and a fourth knocked senseless by a buffalo; but what Landucci especially deplored was that, in the presence of 40,000 women and children, a mare was loosed with a stallion.

Sometimes, for the sake of variety, there would be a sham assault on a wooden castle. In such cases the actors lost control and even killed each other. Fortunately, as we know, there were more innocent amusements like the *calcio*, a sort of football, in which one played less with the feet than the fists. This became a regular sport, with formal rules.

But the most popular diversion, the sport *par excellence*, was the *palio*. Immediately after dinner all the women, decked out in their finery and covered with flowers and jewels, took their children to some point in the street along which the horses would pass. Three strokes of the bell in the great tower of the Signoria were the starting-signal; whereupon the horses would leap forward, bearing the insignia of their owners, who were sometimes great lords from distant cities. The race-track traversed the city in its full length, from the Porta al Prato to the Porta Santa Croce. The magistrates who judged the race sat at the finishing-post. After which the *palio*, which was the prize, was set on a four-wheeled car, adorned with a lion at each corner. This *palio* consisted of a piece of crimson fabric, trimmed with fur and having a fringe of gold and silk, and it was worth three hundred florins.

The custom arose later of making the horses race without jockeys. Sometimes they would break into the line of spectators, when the city would pay for the damage. But the *palio* was too popular to be abandoned. There was even, on the festival of St James, a water-palio, with boats on the Arno; and bitter was the disappointment if there was not enough water in the stream.

The Theatre Develops

The theatre had for long remained exclusively religious. A *sacra rappresentazione*[7] took place in a church, or cloisters, or a refectory, or in the open, and the actors were young boys who belonged to a religious association and who had been trained by the *festaiuoli*. These *impresarii* expended their ingenuity in devising scenery and stage-machinery. There would, for example, be a sky filled with moving figures, lights which came on and went out as in a lightning-flash, a celestial sphere with two companies of angels flying round it, and from which the archangel Gabriel descended in a machine shaped like an almond—a pretty invention of Brunelleschi's.[8]

The torture and execution of martyrs were also represented: St Apollonia,[9] when the executioner broke all her teeth, St Margaret,[10] tied to the stake and crying out: 'Now I rise to a higher station, like gold which is refined in the furnace.' And people admired the fervour of St Barbara,[11] who, when confined in a tower

7. sacred representation   8. Florentine sculptor and architect (1377–1446)   9. martyr who was killed during the persecution of Decius (ca. 248)   10. martyr who refused to recant her faith in order to marry   11. martyr whose father had her killed for being a Christian

with only two windows, pierced a third one, so zealous a believer was she in the Holy Trinity.

The public did not feel out of its element when an angel advanced to explain the action by way of prologue. The actors were like the spectators, belonged to the same age, shot with bow-and-arrow, drank Trebbiano,[12] paid in florins and were familiar with the inns of the *Buco* and the *Panico*.

All this was very innocent. In the 'sacred representation' of Nebuchadnezzar, one saw the sculptor Donatello summoned by the king of Nineveh, who had sent his seneschal to the studio.

'Master, I inform you that you are to appear before our king.'

'What does that mean? I haven't a moment's rest. I have to deliver a pulpit for Prato.'

'You must come at once.'

'I cannot refuse, but I have to carve the *Dovizia* (Abundance) which will be set on a column in the market-place, and for the next quarter of an hour, I cannot undertake more work.' Such dialogue was well-calculated to please the artisan.

As time went by, the stage became definitely secular, pagan and realistic. Machiavelli's *Mandragora*, which was presented in 1526 by the 'Company of the Trowel'; enables one to see how absolutely the tone had changed. The plot is far from edifying: a husband stupidly lending a hand to his marital misfortune, a casuistical monk, and, in the wife only, a rather half-hearted virtue. But this new kind of play was completely successful. The Florentines adored anything witty, astute or farcical, any ingenious ways of getting out of a difficulty. And Machiavelli achieved a similar success when, in the garden of his friend Fornaciaio, he produced the *Clizia*, a play imitated from Plautus.[13] The garden had been levelled so as to allow of a stage, artists were engaged to paint the scenery, and the play was followed by a banquet of which all classes partook, patricians, burghers and common people. The fame of this performance spread all over Tuscany, and even as far as Lombardy.

As the theatre became more exquisite, greater attention was paid to the wardrobe. It was popular now to attire the actresses as nymphs, in a blouse of crimson damask and a skirt of fine Cyprus fabric encrusted with gold, and raised half-way up the

12. white wine   13. Roman playwright (254–184 B.C.)

leg. They wore a garland of flowers and leaves round their heads, and carried a bow, with a quiver suspended behind the shoulder. These pastorals were accompanied by songs, now sentimental, now even free and hearty:

'With water from the fountain, my brunette bathes her face and tender breast.'

'Come, fair neighbours, attired in your skirts of white linen, come from plain and valley, from hill and mountain top, dance with joy and gaily bound, and strew your roses all around.'

Or again, in a different vein: 'O my goddess, appear at thy casement, show me thy angel face, bring thy Taddeo a bowl of soup and a slice of salt pork.'

Poliziano,[14] Pulci[15] and Lorenzo himself composed some of these songs. And what conferred a peculiar lustre on the entertainment was that every class shared in it, everyone understood the bearing and symbolism of the show, whether historical, mythical or political. . . .

Another and exceedingly popular spectacle was the 'Triumph'. The chariot, which plays a great part in the *Divine Comedy* (Beatrice[16] rides in one) and which symbolized the triumph, was perhaps at the origin of the custom. These displays, in any event, became more numerous in the course of time and acquired a more secular character. Rival societies displayed the utmost ingenuity in presenting allegorical triumphs. One would figure the three ages of man; another, the ages of the world symbolized by episodes from Roman history. During the Carnival, which went on for days and days, there would be a series of processions, with a swarm of masked participants, on foot or on horseback, escorting the chariots. The latter bore the figures of Jealousy with four faces armed with spectacles, the four Temperaments and their corresponding planets, the three Fates, and Prudence on a throne with Hope and Fear in chains at her feet.

Mythology was held in honour. Eros[17] appeared at the Carnival as a child in swaddling clothes, blindfolded and with multicoloured wings; while Bacchus,[18] Ariadne[19] and Paris[20] were ac-

---

14. poet, humanist, and teacher (1454–1494)   15. Florentine poet (1432–1484)   16. character who initiates Dante's trip to Hades   17. Greek god of love   18. Roman god of wine   19. daughter of King Midas   20. Trojan prince who started the Trojan War

companied by hunters, nymphs, beggars, hermits, astrologers and devils, all chanting in chorus songs that were gay or moving, and sometimes obscene. And then would come the refrain proper to the Carnival:

'How fair is youth! and, alas, how fleeting! Let him who will, rejoice! For what will the morrow bring us?'

Religion and Honor

CHAPTER
4

Chapter Preface

The Renaissance was an era plagued by religious unrest. The Catholic Church, which had been a dominant cultural force throughout the Middle Ages, was in decline. Its power had eroded and the papacy had recently been hounded by disputes. In 1305 pressure from the French king, Philip IV, resulted in the College of Cardinals, a group of the highest-ranking cardinals in the church, electing a French pope, Clement V. Instead of moving to Rome, the traditional seat of the papacy, Clement never left southern France, settling in Avignon. This outraged the rest of Europe, who believed that Philip IV would unduly influence the pope. However, little could be done due to France's power, and the papacy stayed in France for most of the fourteenth century. Eventually, the demands of France's opponents led to the appointing of a second pope in Rome. Called the Great Schism of 1381, this situation further weakened the Catholic Church by creating a division in power. The church for so long had followed one leader; now it had to choose between two politically allied popes. In 1409 the College of the Cardinals convened a meeting to deal with the schism. Their proposed solution was to depose both "political" popes and appoint a new pope in Rome. This solution did more damage to the papacy, however, as the power of the pope was now suspect, since a council could remove him at will.

Finally, in 1417 a single pope was agreed upon and the papacy was reestablished in Rome. The papacy attempted to return to its position of preeminence and power. The popes of the Renaissance used the considerable wealth of the church to build beautiful cathedrals and commission great works of art. However, one thing the new popes did not avoid was the pattern of corruption that was established in the Middle Ages. Popes took bribes to appoint unqualified individuals to important church positions. They also used church funds to lavish gifts on members of their own families.

The popes of the Renaissance eventually recovered from the political struggles of the schism and became more influential in politics, art, and culture, but they were never able to return the church to its position of primacy in the lives of the people. Though many attended mass and special feasts, the church no longer figured prominently in all aspects of their lives. With the loss of its place at the center of culture and personal life, the church strove to remain a political power. Its great wealth and connections allowed it to continue as a major player in the society of the day; however, its trouble in the spiritual realm would continue. Throughout the Renaissance, popes sought to reform the abuses and corruption of the church, as others followed in the pattern of abusing the power and wealth they controlled. This fluctuation brought the depths of corruption into stark relief when compared with the lofty ideals and goals of reform. Many began to call out for lasting changes to the form and function of the church. In the early sixteenth century, the situation became tense. After several dubious popes, Leo X was elected in 1513. He spent much of his time holding elaborate ceremonies and hunting in the countryside, ignoring the pressing problems of the church. In 1517 a monk and teacher named Martin Luther posted Ninety-five Theses, or statements, on the door of a church in Wittenberg, Germany. These statements called into question the corrupt practices of the church and began a movement called the Protestant Reformation. This movement would grow into a church that would rival the Catholic Church and split Christendom in two.

The legacy of the Catholic Church of the Renaissance is one of impressive cathedrals, crowned with the glory of incredible sculpture and painting, which pointed to a bygone era of power and prestige. The Catholic Church survived the changes of the Renaissance, but the institution that emerged at the end of the age was vastly different from the one that began it.

Moral Codes of the Renaissance

Elizabeth S. Cohen and Thomas V. Cohen

In this overview of the various moral codes that governed daily life in Renaissance Italy, noted historians Elizabeth S. Cohen and Thomas V. Cohen look at two seemingly contrasting influences: the concept of personal honor and religion's moral dictates. While explaining how each affected the culture of the day in different ways and through different means, the authors seek to show not only the differences but also how these two codes complement each other.

Personal honor, which consisted of "unwritten" rules, was based on a set of loyalties: to truth, self, family, and state. Though the particulars of honor were unwritten, it was well known and highly regarded. Religion, on the other hand, was based on a strict written code, which was clearly spelled out for all. It stood in contrast to the pride and judgment of personal honor and called for adherents to live in peace and love.

Although it might appear that religion, with its state-approved, church-controlled code, would dominate the society, honor often trumped religion in daily practice. The two seem contradictory and unable to coexist, but both were strongly valued by the Italians, and both had their place and their purpose.

T he hierarchies and solidarities of Italian society lived in complex symbiosis with its moral values. There, as in any place and time, institutions fostered values that in their turn propped up institutions, in ways so tightly woven that we can hardly say which shaped the other more. Also, as in many cultures, ethical codes were multiple and not always mutually consistent. So how did Renaissance Italians, given their complex and often contradictory values, choose a course of action?

Conflicting moral codes give elbow room to agency. The ca-

Elizabeth S. Cohen and Thomas V. Cohen, *Daily Life in Renaissance Italy*. Westport, CT: Greenwood Press, 2001. Copyright © 2001 by Elizabeth S. Cohen and Thomas V. Cohen. All rights reserved. Reproduced by permission of Greenwood Publishing Group, Inc., Westport, CT.

pacity to choose even while constrained, agency thrives on contradictions, for moral values do not dictate choice, but only help draw boundaries to the set of choices one may make. They set a price and a reward to every option, making some courses cheap, others expensive or quite prohibitive. The complexity that tangles our analysis actually simplifies everyday life, for multiple codes and conflicting moral strictures can liberate. Often one must choose between two goods, or two evils. This fact, though it burdens the choosing, gives us humans leeway, or agency, that no servile computer ever enjoys. Moral dissonance sparks discussion and eases bargaining, two activities central to Renaissance Italian life.

A caution is in order as we survey Renaissance ethics. Moderns looking at the past sometimes mistake moral rules for inviolable commands, as consistent, as logical, and as peremptory as a computer program. They query, for instance, the sensuality of some Renaissance popes or Christian cruelty to Jews and Muslims. "How could they do such a thing? It was against their values!" They expect past peoples to be far more consistent in precepts and conduct than we ever are. Premodern [prior to the Enlightenment] Italians held deeply the values that guided their choices. Yet their behavior corresponded to these rules in as mixed and nuanced a way as does our own conduct when it heeds our moral strictures.

In premodern Italy, two elaborate, very sweeping moral systems contradicted one another on almost every point: a code of honor and Christian virtue. So contrary were they that, at first glance, one might expect Renaissance Italians to have spent their days baffled and torn. Honor urged vengeance, pride, display, and partisan loyalties, all deplored by religion. Religion, meanwhile, preached peace, mercy, and humility and a universalizing social ethic, at odds with honor's deep particularism. Yet Italians absorbed these contradictions readily, for reasons that we shall explore. Alongside these first two ethics were other, less sweeping, but still potent moral codes, anchored in the law and in the customs of family and of group solidarity. These complicated the picture yet further.

Of the two competing chief Renaissance codes, the Christian ethic had the far sharper, more coherent formulation, and perhaps a prior claim to attention and adherence, backed as it was by the potent institutions of the church, a rich intellectual tradition of theological speculation, and God himself, who to enforce good behavior held souls hostage. Yet it was honor that often shaped everyday morality. Not formally encoded or written down and open to wiry adaptation from case to case, honor was learned, practiced, and enforced in the endless routine or extraordinary exchanges of daily life. Therefore, we start our discussion there and then use this largely tacit secular code as a foil for the more explicit religious morality inscribed in treatises, preached from pulpits, and taught in the confessional.

Honor in Society

Rather than a formal code of behavior, honor was a set of practices and a logic. Renaissance Italian habits had much in common with a larger cultural complex known as Mediterranean honor that anthropologists have argued about at length. While this pattern has many variants and no clear boundaries in time and space, these concepts help us grab hold of an elusive but central structure of premodern Italian mentality. Its characteristic elements included prickly male pride, violent revenge, suspicion of outsiders, a sharp distinction between males and females, and fierce male responsibility for female chastity. At its core, honor was a social quality, the distillation of reputation. As such, it was external to the self. It existed in the thoughts of casual onlookers who appraised you, as well as in the judgments of the perduring circle of family and friends who monitored your doings. So potent was this bearing of witness that often others' judgment must have seemed to constitute one's very self. In this way, honor acquired also an inward aspect. Knowing that you had acted so that others approved underlay an inner self-esteem. While praise left a glow of satisfaction, probably more acute was the sting of public scorn. This inner anguish that we call "shame," the Italians called *vergogna*. This term had a triple meaning—at once a state of mind, a painful social purgatory, and a capacity of soul. The first is acute embarrassment, the second passing or permanent disgrace. The third merits further examination. In Italian eyes, a person whose soul was "without shame" (*senza vergogna*) would not flinch in the face of public reproof and therefore behaved outrageously. Such people either did not know the rules or simply chose to flout them; they lacked honor.

As a quality of soul, honor, Italians thought, inhered in persons, as a kind of moral potential. "He is a man of honor." Here, the male pronoun fits, for female honor differed. Honor, in this sense, was virtue—any virtue. Nevertheless, certain good qualities more pertained. Paramount was fidelity to word. A person of honor would tell the truth. His reports about the past and present were faithful; his promises about the future held good. The same attitudes applied here as in the torture chamber; truth telling was a luxury, indulged only by those who could afford its costs. A person of honor, the logic went, would keep promises, however expensive, and give true reports, however painful or embarrassing. A weakling would twist the truth. Thus, honesty signaled prosperity and strength. A second virtue, also closely tied to wealth and power, was generosity. This took two forms: largesse and magnanimity. Largesse was open-handedness. One gave gifts, and offered food and hospitality. Magnanimity, as the Latin roots (*magna* and *anima*) reveal, was greatness of soul. The magnanimous person, usually male, forgave enemies and generously forbore vexation. The last chief virtue was courage. All these qualities, fundamentally male, descended from the ethics of the medieval warrior class. Women too might derive honor from their possession, yet the essence of female honor lay elsewhere.

For women especially, and often for children and dependent young men as well, honor, as virtue, often hinged less on what one did than on what one refrained from. Self-restraint garnered praise. This self-checking looked like a kind of voluntary shame, a self-imposed sensitivity to the judgment of others. Its serene effect reversed that of *vergogna*, the involuntary shame imposed by disapproval. Italians called this good shame *pudore*, just what the "im-pudent" lacked. In women and subordinate males, the marks of good-shame were a quiet bearing, modestly downcast eyes, and a self-conscious, virtuous blush. . . .

Challenging Honor

The agonism [competitive spirit] so typical of social life provoked many contests for honor, for honor was often best won at the expense of others. One could steal it. To Italian minds, it was rare—

a limited good. That is, like land and wealth in an economy that grew slowly if at all, it seemed a conspicuously finite resource, best gained by depriving others. The scarcities of land and goods were concrete and necessary; that of honor, however, followed no iron laws of supply and demand. Clearly, there could be only one first place in line, one high table at the banquet, one ruler, and one general of the troops, but other honors—a prince's favor, knighthood, a city's praise, a university degree—could multiply. Supply was elastic, economists would say. But all such things had to remain rare or risk debasement.

Struggles for scarce honor involved individuals and groups alike, for both it and shame were contagious. One caught them from the company one kept. Collectivities—cities, trades, professions, neighborhoods, patrons, and above all families—had a notional shared honor that they imparted to their members. The glory, or the disgrace, of the whole in some sense touched the parts. This fact inspired proud display, manly swagger, and much legal and political jostling over what might seem minor adjustments to seating at table or a line of march. There was group dishonor in yielding place, especially if pressed. Many tumultuous and often bloody conflicts of daily life stemmed from struggles not over tangibles but over reputation. In this, what held true for groups held too for persons.

A challenge put honor into question; it put it up for stealing. To refuse the contest was shameful; one lost at once. But to take up the challenge was to stake one's reputation. All sorts of exchanges followed such a logic. Since a man's honor resided in the integrity of his reputation, house, property, body, and womenfolk, all sorts of slights, incursions, assaults, and amorous innuendo could be read as challenges to honor. The interpretation of such moments was elastic; if witnesses agreed that there had been affront, a man had to counterattack or lose standing. . . .

One mark of male strength was the capacity to tell the truth. Honor and honesty vouched for one another. Accordingly, the directest way to challenge a man was to call him a liar. The insult: "Cheating coward!" The riposte: "You are lying through your throat!" At that, out came the daggers. So routine were such exchanges that, as in Shakespeare's England, one called this usual challenge "giving the lie." The formal duel, a sixteenth-century refinement on the age-old brawl, almost always pre-served this step.

Other challenges were just as likely as "giving the lie" to pro-voke a violent response. Shakespeare caught one Italian folkway in *Romeo and Juliet*: "Do you bite your thumb at me sir?" In fact, any finger would do. . . .

Honor and Standing in Society

Hierarchy was tightly linked to honor; high status both conferred it and set boundaries to its contests. At the same time, honor per-vaded the whole social order. Underlings, even peasants, thieves, and prostitutes, possessed a strong sense of it, but only among their peers. In their struggles for face and standing, they could not aspire to filch honor from their social betters. Nor could their superiors take honor from them. Rather, contests for honor in-volved near-equals. A gentleman could afford to shrug off an in-sult by an inferior; indeed, to take it to heart was to stoop and risk derision. Or he could avenge it by some scornful act that in-flicted pain and shame without engaging his own honor. This was what Hamlet meant by "the proud man's contumely." Cer-tainly one would never challenge an underling; that would have looked bizarre. Honor usually came into agonistic play among peers, be they lords or stable hands, where real adjustments to prestige could happen. Thus, as a social practice, honor, both ex-pressed and supported Renaissance hierarchy; as an ethic, it was conservative. It also reinforced countless solidarities, for, by its combative ethos, it attached men and women to their groups. . . .

Religion as a Moral Code

In its social conservatism and its respect for power and privilege, the honor ethic diverged from Christian morality, which had a subversive streak that often undercut both lay values and many institutions that governed Italian life. This tension between sacred ethics and everyday life was ancient and was and is in many ways peculiar to Christianity. In Italy, where faith encountered life's needs and pleasures, struggle often ensued. Religion urged against warfare and internecine strife—peace; against satisfying desire—chastity; against feeding hunger—periodic fasting; against a Sun-day spent at wine and gaming in the tavern or at rounds of mallet ball—sober church attendance; against the strategies of lineage—fat bequests to churches, respect for monastic vocations, and no divorcing a barren wife. The confrontation led to compromises and nuanced adaptations on both sides. Moreover, faith was only partially subversive, for it relied on and sanctified the very institutions—family and state—that it also hedged and chided.

Honor had no church; in this respect, Christianity differed hugely. Behind everyday Catholic morality stood a vast, complex, sophisticated, immensely wealthy institution of great prestige. The church not only embodied a morality but propagated and enforced it in pulpit, confessional, school, and court of law. Honor versus piety: no contest! Or so one might think, but honor not only thrived but even often hogged center stage. All Italians except the Jews adhered to the faith, but many lent only half a heart to Christian ethics. Therefore, put aside the enduring delusions of many dreary films about supposedly embattled individualism and fanatical, oppressive monks, that the medieval church was a bit like God: omniscient, omnipotent, ubiquitous, all but eternal, and relentlessly meddlesome. Such modern fantasies, which often project onto Catholicism a mixture of the KGB [intelligence agency of the former Soviet Union] and high school assistant principal, profoundly misconstrue a complex institution. The church, for all that it had a government in Rome, a chain of command, and, for the times, efficient lines of communication, remained a polycentric institution. There was ample room for local initiative, and its many members often walked different paths, worked at cross-purposes, or quarreled. Only after the Council of Trent (1545–63) [council of the Roman Catholic Church convened to deal with the Protestant Reformation] did the center tighten its hold on the whole. The modern Roman church therefore owes much of its present structure to its response to the Protestant challenge. And not even Trent brought unanimity.

The separation of sacred and profane, and of church and world, though central to the Christian vision, could never be complete. Students often write as if the church stood outside society's tent, barking orders through the flaps. Nothing was ever so simple. Christianity was itself of two minds about the virtues of being in or out; the monastic impulse had always hankered after separation, but social activism plunged deep in. And "church" itself, in its original Greek (*ekklesia*), meant "gathering" and hence community, not of clergy alone but of all the faithful; the notion was inclusive, not separatist. Furthermore, Christian institutions had political and economic functions that embroiled them in practical affairs. Also, while the clergy were indeed legally a separate order, they did not have sole control of Christian organizations. There was much lay initiative—on committees overseeing parish property, in confraternities, pilgrimages, and festivals to mark holy days. And Renaissance Italian clergymen, to the annoyance of assorted church reformers, were notoriously quick, as they politicked for good appointments, to remember their alliances with their families and friends. Thus, much of the debate about religious reform, in the sixteenth century as in the Middle Ages, turned on the issue of how hard one should or could campaign to separate the church from the entanglements and pleasures of the world.

By what medium did the church inculcate values that bore on everyday life? The routes were many. Before Trent, the Roman church as a whole did not put a teaching mission first. Priests as a rule did not preach; they provided sacraments, watched over their churches, and, as peacemakers, brokered social relationships. Only after Trent's reform of the parish clergy did they turn to instructing the laity. Until then, they did confess their flocks, but seldom more than once a year, at Easter. Nor did monks preach; their job was collective prayer, good liturgy, hospitality, and sometimes care for the sick, pilgrims, and the poor. But preaching there was, and it was enormously influential. The task fell to the friars, Franciscans [order of friars who followed the rule of St. Francis] and Dominicans [order of friars who followed the rule of St. Dominic] above all, who from the thirteenth century on routinely toured the cities and towns of Italy. To the laity, preachers taught doctrine, but especially morality and devotional practice. In an age where information was scarce, the friars combined the roles of entertainers, broadcasters, inspirers, prophets, and scolds. When gifted, they succeeded hugely; a good preacher could draw thousands and hold them for four hours at a stretch. A truly charismatic one, like Bernardino of Siena [Franciscan preacher who travelled around Italy] or Savonarola [Dominican preacher who spoke out against vice in Florence] was a political force to reckon with. Such men could evangelize a city, bringing about, for a while, dramatic changes in public and private behavior. But preaching was not the church's only conduit for ethics; there were several others. Uplifting books inspired and nagged the better educated. Especially after Trent, schools for the poor taught catechism alongside the ABCs. Confraternities, under lay control but usually linked to priests, practiced devotions, did good works, and paraded solemnly on holidays. Christian art, some of it narrative and much of it didactic, ornamented houses, street-corner shrines, and countless churches and chapels. Italians recognized their familiar saints, posing with their standard emblems, and picked out readily the famous incidents from the lives of Jesus and of Mary and other familiar sacred stories. Alongside all these channels belonging to or sponsored by the church were others purely social; that is, in ways at once self-evident and very hard to document, Italians imbibed Christian values from one another. Moral examples, precepts, chidings, stories, proverbs, turns of speech, movements of the hands, the head, the body could all impart a religious ethic that, like honor, was deeply embedded in the practices of everyday life. . . .

Other Moral Codes

Tempting as it is to reduce Renaissance Italian life to a restless dialogue between two ill-matched moralities, in truth the picture was more complex. There were other ethics on the scene as well, subcodes more limited in scope and weight but still influential. One of the most pervasive was the law. Renaissance Italy had a rich legal tradition, with intellectual roots in ancient Roman codes, church law, old Germanic legislation, and feudal practices. In towns and country alike, Italians were inured to dealing with the courts and to running to notaries, scribes, secretaries, chancellors, and other officials. All such men purveyed legal language and ideas. The law offered notions of equity, impartiality, due recompense, respect for form, proper consent and consultation, verification, fair arbitration, conditional and unconditional assent or agreement; its terminology infiltrated the speech of every social class. In general, like religion, the law bolstered the notion of a public interest. In this idea, it countered honor's moral particularism, advancing the principle of a more abstract, impartial fairness, guaranteed by due process. Besides the law, there were also other rhetorics, closely tied to family, professions, and other solidarities and to neighborhood. These discourses had much to do with roles: the love of parents, the loving obedience of sons and daughters and the loyalty of servants, the solidarity of colleagues, and the mutual help and discretion of neighbors, who, despite their vigilant surveillance of good local order, should never stick their noses in other people's business. This last double injunction was flatly contradictory. It reminds us once more that no moral code, large or small, is ever internally consistent. Whatever unity any set of values possessed was thematic, more rhetoric than logic. A precious larger lesson for historians, often overlooked, is that, however much past values illuminate some bygone time, they never fully explain its actions.

A Father Encourages His Son to Live Honorably

Lorenzo de Medici

Lorenzo de Medici (1449–1492) was a member of the ruling family of Florence. After assuming leadership from his father, Cosimo, in 1469, he sought to establish Florence and the Medici family as even greater forces in Italy. Known as a great patron of the arts, Lorenzo commissioned works from Leonardo da Vinci, Michelangelo, and others. He was known to the Florentines as Lorenzo the Magnificent, a title bestowed on him due to his excellent leadership and care of the people.

In the following letter, Lorenzo is writing to his son, Giovanni, who has just been named a cardinal at age fourteen. While many sons and nephews of wealthy families gained such posts very early in life, Giovanni was the youngest ever. His father had worked hard to gain the appointment, which he saw as broadening the Medici power base. Lorenzo wrote a letter of instruction to his son to guide him as he moved to Rome to begin his duties.

The Catholic Church at the time was going through a transition. Many were calling for reform of political and financial abuses that were taking place. This letter shows a strange contrast that existed at the time: Even as Lorenzo is calling his son to stay above the corruption and improper dealings of the church, his very appointment at age fourteen owes itself to those precepts. As a picture of Renaissance impropriety in appointing a youth to the second highest religious office in the Western world, this letter offers a look at how honor and religion often worked in contrast to each other, even as they worked in concert. Lorenzo sought to bring honor to his family through the appointment, and then encouraged his son to bring propriety to the church through proper conduct.

This letter offers a fascinating opportunity to look at the in-

Lorenzo de Medici, "Lorenzo De Medici: Paternal Advice to a Cardinal (c. 1491)," *Source-Book of the Italian Renaissance*, edited and translated by Merrick Whitcomb. Philadelphia: University of Pennsylvania Press, 1903.

134

terplay between honor and religion and to see how easily the people of the time could move between the two, even while dealing with one particular situation.

You, and all of us who are interested in your welfare, ought to esteem ourselves highly favored by Providence, not only for the many honors and benefits bestowed upon our house, but more particularly for having conferred upon us, in your person, the greatest dignity we have ever enjoyed. This favor, in itself so important, is rendered still more so by the circumstances with which it is accompanied, and especially by the consideration of your youth and of our situation in the world. The first that I would therefore suggest to you is that you ought to be grateful to God, and continually to recollect that it is not through your merits, your prudence, or your solicitude, that this event has taken place, but through his favor, which you can only repay by a pious, chaste and exemplary life; and that your obligations to the performance of these duties are so much the greater, as in your early years you have given some reasonable expectations that your riper age may produce such fruits. It would indeed be highly disgraceful, and as contrary to your duty as to my hopes, if, at a time when others display a greater share of reason and adopt a better mode of life, you should forget the precepts of your youth, and forsake the path in which you have hitherto trodden. Endeavor, therefore, to alleviate the burden of your early dignity by the regularity of your life and by your perseverance in those studies which are suitable to your profession. It gave me great satisfaction to learn, that, in the course of the past year, you had frequently, of your own accord, gone to communion and confession; nor do I conceive that there is any better way of obtaining the favor of heaven than by habituating yourself to a performance of these and similar duties. This appears to me to be the most suitable and useful advice which, in the first instance, I can possibly give you.

Avoid Temptations and Be an Example

I well know, that as you are now to reside in Rome, that sink of all iniquity, the difficulty of conducting yourself by these admonitions will be increased. The influence of example is itself prevalent; but you will probably meet with those who will particularly endeavor to corrupt and incite you to vice; because, as you may yourself perceive, your early attainment to so great a dignity is not observed without envy, and those who could not prevent your receiving that honor will secretly endeavor to diminish it, by inducing you to forfeit the good estimation of the public; thereby precipitating you into that gulf into which they had themselves fallen; in which attempt, the consideration of your youth will give them a confidence of success. To these difficulties you ought to oppose yourself with the greater firmness, as there is at present less virtue amongst your brethren of the college [other cardinals]. I acknowledge indeed that several of them are good and learned men, whose lives are exemplary, and whom I would recommend to you as patterns of your conduct. By emulating them you will be so much the more known and esteemed, in proportion as your age and the peculiarity of your situation will distinguish you from your colleagues. Avoid, however, as you would Scylla or Charybdis [sea monsters in Homer's *Odyssey*] the imputation of hypocrisy; guard against all ostentation, either in your conduct or your discourse; affect not austerity, nor ever appear too serious. This advice you will, I hope, in time understand and practice better than I can express it.

Yet you are not unacquainted with the great importance of the character which you have to sustain, for you well know that all the Christian world would prosper if the cardinals were what they ought to be; because in such a case there would always be a good pope, upon which the tranquility of Christendom so materially depends. Endeavor then to render yourself such, that if all the rest resembled you, we might expect this universal blessing. To give you particular directions as to your behavior and conversation would be a matter of no small difficulty. I shall, therefore, only recommend, that in your intercourse with the cardinals and other men of rank, your language be unassuming and respectful, guiding yourself, however, by your own reason, and not submitting to be impelled by the passions of others, who, actuated by improper motives, may pervert the use of their reasons. Let it satisfy your conscience that your conversation is without intentional offense; and if, through impetuosity of temper, any one should be offended, as his enmity is without just cause, so it will not be very lasting. On this your first visit to Rome, it will, however, be more advisable for you to listen to others than to speak much yourself.

You are now devoted to God and the church: on which account you ought to aim at being a good ecclesiastic, and to shew that you prefer the honor and state of the church and of the apostolic see to every other consideration. Nor, while you keep this in view, will it be difficult for you to favor your family and your native place. On the contrary, you should be the link to bind this city closer to the church, and our family with the city; and although it be impossible to foresee what accidents may happen, yet I doubt not but this may be done with equal advantage to all: observing, however, that you are always to prefer the interests of the church.

Live a Prudent Life

You are not only the youngest cardinal in the college, but the youngest person that ever was raised to that rank; and you ought, therefore, to be the most vigilant and unassuming, not giving others occasion to wait for you, either in the chapel, the consistory [assembly of cardinals] or upon deputations. You will soon get a sufficient insight into the manners of your brethren. With those of less respectable character converse not with too much intimacy; not merely on account of the circumstance in itself, but for the sake of public opinion. Converse on general topics with all. On public occasions, let your equipage and address be rather below than above mediocrity. A handsome house and a well-ordered family will be preferable to a great retinue and a splendid residence. Endeavor to live with regularity, and gradually to bring your expenses within those bounds which in a new establishment cannot perhaps be expected. Silk and jewels are not suitable for persons in your station. Your taste will be better shown in the acquisition of a few elegant remains of antiquity, or in the collecting of handsome books, and by your attendants being learned and well-bred rather than numerous. Invite others to your house oftener than you receive invitations. Practise neither too frequently. Let your own food be plain, and take sufficient exercise, for those who wear your habit are soon liable, without great caution, to contract infirmities. The station of a cardinal is not less secure than elevated; on which account those who arrive at it too frequently become negligent; conceiving their object is attained and that they can preserve it with little trouble, This idea is often injurious to the life and character of those who entertain it. Be attentive, therefore, to your conduct, and confide in others too little rather than too much. There is one rule which I would recommend to your attention in preference to all others. Rise early in the morning. This will not only contribute to your health, but will enable you to arrange and expedite the business of the day; and as there are various duties incident to your station, such as the performance of divine service, studying, giving audience, and so forth, you will find the observance of this admonition productive of the greatest utility. Another very necessary precaution, particularly on your entrance into public life, is to deliberate every evening on what you may have to perform the following day, that you may not be unprepared for whatever may happen.

Conduct with Other Cardinals and the Pope

With respect to your speaking in the consistory, it will be most becoming for you at present to refer the matters in debate to the judgment of his holiness [the pope] alleging as a reason your own youth and inexperience. You will probably be desired to intercede for the favors of the pope on particular occasions. Be cautious, however, that you trouble him not too often; for his temper leads him to be most liberal to those who weary him least with their solicitations. This you must observe, lest you should give him offense, remembering also at times to converse with him on more agreeable topics; and if you should be obliged to request some kindness from him, let it be done with that modesty and humility which are so pleasing to his disposition. Farewell.

The Role of the Church in Daily Life

Gene Brucker

Gene Brucker, a professor of history at the University of California, Berkeley, has written several books on the Renaissance and specifically the city of Florence. In this piece, he examines the role the church played in day-to-day life during the Renaissance.

While rejecting claims that the church either ruled the culture with an iron fist or was rendered irrelevant by the secularizing influence of the humanist movement, Brucker seeks to give a more balanced view. He points to the high church attendance rates that crossed social and economic boundaries to prove religion's importance. It was not uncommon for people to attend both morning mass and the evening vesper service daily, not to mention Sunday masses and special feasts and festivals, of which Florence observed more than forty per year.

The church in the Renaissance was involved in every aspect of daily life. As a political and economic force at the time, its influence was not limited to the spiritual realm.

O utwardly, the Florentine church of the fifteenth century resembled closely the institution which St. Francis had known two centuries earlier. It was still overwhelmingly a medieval church architecturally; the classicism of the Renaissance had scarcely made an impact. Florence's medieval church was active, busy, noisy and colorful; the Renaissance church retained all of these qualities. It was a church of large and frequent processions through the streets, sweeping up clergy and laity in their wake. It was a church of begging friars making their rounds, and also of distinguished scholars like the Augustinian Luigi Marsili and the Dominican friar and saint, Antonino. Its symbols and monuments were visible everywhere: the street corner crucifix and

Gene Brucker, *Renaissance Florence*. Berkeley: University of California Press, 1983. Copyright © 1969 by John Wiley & Sons, Inc. Supplements copyright © 1983 by The Regents of the University of California. Reproduced by permission.

the Virgin's illuminated portrait; the small, cramped parish church and the grandiose monastic foundation. The church touched the life of every Florentine at frequent intervals and on several levels. Its most notable characteristics were its ubiquity and its pervasiveness.

Owing to the active participation of the laity in cult ceremonies, the secular and ecclesiastical worlds were in regular and intimate communication. Attendance at morning mass and evening vesper service was a standard part of the daily routine of many Florentines. The clergy officiated at baptisms, marriages, and burials; they were often witnesses to the last testaments dictated by the moribund. Many wills contained elaborate and detailed provisions for masses to be recited for the souls of the testator and his family. The implementation of these bequests forced their heirs to maintain close contact with the clergy, who were charged with this responsibility. How demanding this burden might become for a conscientious executor is revealed in a 1377 testament—by no means unique—made by Francesco Niccoli. This merchant bequeathed some real estate to the Augustinian convent of S. Spirito in Florence, "with the proviso that the friars of the chapter are required to celebrate mass every morning in perpetuity, in which they shall pray to God for the soul of the testator and his relatives; and also that every year in perpetuity on the feast day of the Virgin Mary, they shall celebrate a mass, in which they must light twelve candles . . . and in this chapel in perpetuity there shall be lighted a lamp both day and night." Niccoli further stipulated that if these provisions were not fulfilled, the bequest was to be withdrawn from S. Spirito and the property given to the society of Orsanmichele "to be expended by that society on the paupers of Christ for the soul of the testator."

The Church and Civil Law

Contacts between the religious and lay communities resulted, too, from the church's traditional claim to exercise jurisdiction and control over a broad range of secular activities. In Florence, with its complex economic structure, the problem of usury was particularly acute. Episcopal courts normally did not prosecute suspected usurers during their lifetime, but waited to bring suit against the estate of the deceased. Since these court records have not survived, it is impossible to estimate the incidence of usury prosecutions. Other sources provide fragments of evidence about a handful of cases, all involving businessmen of considerable wealth. In a letter written in 1385 to a relative living abroad, Domenico Lanfredini described his quarrel with the bishop over this issue: "After the death of my parents and my brother, the bishop initiated a process against Sandro's [his father's] estate, accusing him of usury. This has been a source of great embarrassment, and I am still not absolved, nor will I be absolved without loss. . . . There are others at the bishop's court who are claiming the usury which they had paid to Sandro in the past." While these cases were not common, they did remind Florentines that the church possessed the instruments to regulate and penalize their economic activities, even though its surveillance was not as thorough as that of the secular authority.

In the absence of court records, one can only speculate about the number and variety of offenses against canon law which were prosecuted in ecclesiastical tribunals. Heresy cases were the exclusive preserve of the Inquisitor's court; heretics condemned to death were turned over to the secular authorities for punishment. Blasphemy was perhaps the most common misdemeanor for which men were haled before the inquisitor or the bishop's vicar-general; Giovanni Villani[1] once complained about an inquisitor who levied a fine "for every little word which someone wrongly uttered against God." Moral offenses and attacks upon the clergy were violations of both civil and canon law; information on such crimes is abundant in the records of the secular courts. For example, the scion of a prominent mercantile family, Adoardo Peruzzi, was sentenced to death by the podesta[2] in 1400 for conspiring to murder a priest, and for complicity in the assassination of an abbot. One case tried in the court of the vicar of Valdelsa (1413) describes a remarkable variety of sacrilegious acts committed by Antonio di Tome of Castro Tremoleti, "in violation of divine, as well as civil and canon, law." Antonio had incestuous relations with his cousin, by whom he had a child, and also with his niece. In a fit of anger occasioned by his gambling losses, he slashed a painting of the Virgin, and later used his knife to deface

1. banker and merchant who wrote a history of Florence   2. mayor

a coin upon which her image was engraved. For these crimes, Antonio was sentenced to be burned to death in a wooden cage, but this punishment was later changed to decapitation.

The Church and the Wealthy

Some of the bonds connecting the church and lay society involved all groups in the community. Rich and poor alike crowded into parish churches to observe the Host and to receive the spiritual ministrations of the clergy; aristocrats and lowly vagabonds appeared together as defendants in ecclesiastical tribunals. But only the upper stratum of Florentine society was involved in two spheres of contact between the secular and religious worlds, where relations were unusually close and sensitive. These were property and personnel.

Like ecclesiastical structures elsewhere in Catholic Europe, the Florentine church—or more accurately, the various foundations which comprised that church—owned a substantial amount of property in Tuscany. A record of rents and land transactions of the Carthusian[3] monastery near Galluzzo, five miles south of Florence, reveals that the convent's investments were about equally divided between city and countryside. The Certosa's[4] property in the city included a cloth factory in the Via Maggio, a tailor's shop in the Via del Garbo, a barber shop in the parish of S. Piero Gattolino, a dwelling in the Borgo Ogni Santi. Farms and vineyards owned by the Carthusians were scattered throughout Tuscany, and furnished not only such staples as wheat, wine, and oil for the monastic kitchen, but also surpluses for sale in local markets. Elio Conti's[5] recent study of land ownership in twelve *contado*[6] zones reveals two significant facts. First, ecclesiastical foundations owned 13½ percent of the land in these zones in 1427; the figures for individual zones varied from 2 to 45 percent. Second, church ownership increased dramatically in these districts during the century, to 23.2 percent in 1498, with zonal variations from 7 to 60 percent. These figures suggest that the claim made by the republic's ambassador to Rome in 1452, that the church possessed one-third of the real property in Florentine territory, was not a wild exaggeration.

3. order of monks founded by St. Bruno   4. a Carthusian monastery   5. historian who specialized in Renaissance studies   6. peasant

Much of the revenue from ecclesiastical property was expended on quite legitimate objectives: the stipends of parish priests; the subsidy of monasteries, hospitals, and educational institutions; the payment of papal taxes. Some of this income, however, found its way into secular hands, with little or no benefit accruing to the church. For centuries, the Visdomini family had enjoyed certain lucrative rights to the bishop's revenues; the Arrigucci had a similar (but smaller) claim on Fiesole's episcopal *mensa*, an annual subsidy of 120 bushels of grain. Many patrician families had the right of presentation to parish churches in the city, or to baptismal churches (*pievi*) in the *contado*. Sometime in the thirteenth century the Medici acquired patronage rights to the church of S. Tommaso adjacent to the Old Market. The revenues accruing to the family from such livings were usually not large, although they did provide opportunities for granting a modest income to a poor relation or client. Not economic interest but pride induced families to engage in lengthy and expensive litigation to vindicate their patronage rights over a church. It was doubtless for similar reasons that Pandolfo Ricasoli, member of that powerful noble family residing in the Chianti region southeast of Florence, assaulted a priest, Ser Giunta Casini, asserting that "we have done this to you because you have celebrated [mass] in the church of S. Piero de Montegonzi at the request of the parishioners and against the wishes of Albertaccio and Pandolfo [Ricasoli], and if you dare to celebrate mass again, we will kill you."

By 1400, however, these traditional patronage rights had lost much of their value and importance for the Florentine patriciate. More significant were the lucrative benefices[7] and the prominent careers in the ecclesiastical hierarchy which were open to aristocratic clerics with good connections in the Roman curia.[8] In 1342, Giovanni Villani noted that very few of his fellow-citizens had ever entered the College of Cardinals, "since the Florentines make little effort to induce their sons to become clerics." After the Black Death,[9] however, the number of Florentines in holy orders increased substantially. Was this influx the result of

7. a church office that paid a salary and was usually granted to members of influential families   8. ministries and organizations that assist the pope in carrying out the mission of the Catholic Church   9. plague that hit Europe in the fourteenth century

the psychological effects of the plague, of a more intense piety, or rather a desire for economic and professional security? For many of these priests and monks, the church must have seemed an attractive alternative, more stable and more respectable, to a business career with its risks and vicissitudes.

Buying and Selling Church Positions

The traffic in Florentine benefices was no more crassly material-istic than elsewhere; the exploitation of ecclesiastical office by lo-cal aristocracies had been a fact of European life since the fourth century. But in a society so permeated with mercantile values, the economic dimension assumed particular significance. The is-sue is discussed with unusual candor by Lanfredino Lanfredini in a letter to his son in September 1406:

> I write to inform you that your close relative—the Augustinian friar, Maestro Bernardo Angioleri—has been made bishop of Thebes, which is in Romania near Negroponte, with a yearly in-come of 2500 ducats. We are his only kin, and he asked me to send him one of my sons, whom he will treat as his own; he will leave him his estate and procure good benefices for him. So I wrote him about all of you: where you were and what you were doing. He replied that he would particularly like to have you, that he would cherish you and bequeathe you his entire estate. You should know that he is an old man of eighty, distinguished, and very well liked by the Pope and [the members of] the Roman cu-ria. If I may be permitted to advise you, I would urge you to visit him as soon as possible, and see how he treats you.

Normally, benefices did not fall so easily into Florentine hands, but were obtained after long and arduous effort. The correspon-dence of a papal secretary, Francesco Bruni, describes the efforts by Francesco del Bene in 1364 to obtain a local church, S. Maria sopra Porta, for his son Bene, a law student at the University of Bologna. This church was in the papal gift, and competing for the office with Florentine aspirants were curial cardinals who sought the post for their favorites. Besieged by this throng of petitioners, Pope Urban V[10] endeavored to sift out the unworthy and the un-qualified. A commission of cardinals appointed to review candi-dates scrutinized educational requirements, which Bene fulfilled

10. pope from 1362 to 1370

only partially, for he had not yet obtained the doctorate at Bologna. Letters of recommendation were important and Bruni urged Francesco del Bene to obtain testimonials from several sources: papal legates, the governors of the University of Florence, the captains of the Parte Guelfa, and the directors of the Alberti company, who were the leading papal bankers in Avignon in the 1360s. In this competition with five cardinals and several Florentine candidates, Bene del Bene finally obtained the prize. Contributing to his success was the factor of residence, which gave him an advantage over the necessarily absent curialists, but his greatest asset was undoubtedly the influence of Francesco Bruni, who could sway papal judgment in favor of his clients.

This scramble for ecclesiastical office had certain unfortunate consequences; it tended to exacerbate relations between families, particularly if they belonged to rival political factions. Since the middle of the fourteenth century, a group of patrician conservatives identified with the Parte Guelfa had advocated close ties with the papacy and support for papal policy in Italy. Their opponents suspected these men of advocating this course to obtain benefices for their relatives, as Buonaccorso Pitti charged in his quarrel with the Ricasoli over the abbey of Ruota. Two years before the Ruota incident, Pitti had lost another contest for a benefice. While seeking a papal grant of a hospital in Altopascio (near Lucca) for a nephew, he encountered the opposition of Niccolò da Uzzano, an influential member of the papal faction. Although Buonaccorso had been encouraged to apply for this benefice by Cardinal Baldassare Cossa (later Pope John XXIII), the prelate later reneged on his promise to support the Pitti candidacy, since he did not wish to offend Niccolò da Uzzano. The Altopascio and Ruota incidents prompted Buonaccorso to admonish his sons: "Take example from this case wherein we suffered from trying to vie with the powerful, meddling in squabbles over church benefices and getting involved with priests. Have no dealings with them and you will be wise."

For most patrician families, however, the church was too ubiquitous—and too wealthy—to be ignored. No systematic study has been made of the contribution of ecclesiastical resources to the fortunes of particular Florentine families, but scattered evidence suggests that it could be very important. Gregorio Dati admitted that his brother Leonardo, while general of the Dominican order, saved him from bankruptcy with a timely loan which was never repaid. A recently published account book of the Corsini family reveals that during the tenure of Andrea and Neri Corsini as bishops of Fiesole (1348–1377), their relatives took over the management of the episcopal patrimony and exploited it for their economic advantage.

This pattern of intimate and frequent contact between clergy and laity fostered the anticlericalism which was so pervasive in Florence. The hostility which the clergy aroused in the secular mind was probably due less to the occasional scoundrel or blackguard[11] in clerical robes than to the fact that priests and monks were so ubiquitous, so visible. Some of the roots of Florentine (and Italian) anticlericalism can be traced directly to the ambivalent position which the priest occupied in a society still imbued with the primitive values of Europe's feudal age, the values of a warrior nobility. The priest was a figure of contempt because his vows prohibited him from filling the masculine role. But given his peculiarly close relationship with women, he was also in a strategic position to break his vow of chastity, and to deprive the male of two cherished possessions: a virtuous wife and virginal daughters. In yet another sense, the priest was a menace to the lay community. As a man of God, he was a neutral and uncommitted figure in secular affairs; his clerical garb was his badge of innocence and noninvolvement. But whenever he abandoned his neutral posture to join a faction or a cause, he was particularly dangerous, since his movements did not normally arouse suspicion. Priests and monks were often recruited as agents and messengers in conspiracies and assassinations; their complicity in these enterprises intensified the anticlerical feelings among the laity. In appearance so weak and defenseless, the men of God were powerful, privileged, and dangerous.

11. a morally reprehensible person

Chronology

1307–1321

Dante Alighieri (1265–1321) writes *The Divine Comedy*. This is the first major piece of literature written in Italian (most works of the time are produced in Latin).

April 6, 1341

Francesco Petrarch is crowned poet laureate in Rome. Many historians point to this as the beginning of the Renaissance.

1347–1351

The Black Plague hits Europe, killing more than a third of the population.

1397

Giovanni de Medici moves to Florence. The Medici will become the leading family during the Renaissance.

1412

Filippo Brunelleschi (1377–1446) writes *Rules of Perspective*.

1419

Brunelleschi designs the dome of the Florence Cathedral.

1417

The papacy, which had split when it returned to Rome following its time in Avignon, is reunited when a single pope, Pope Martin V, is elected in Rome.

1429

Cosimo de Medici (1389–1464) takes over his father's business and continues to build it.

1433

Donatello (1386–1466) creates his sculpture of *David*.

1434

Cosimo de Medici becomes ruler of Florence.

1447

Nicholas V becomes pope.

1450

Francesco Sforza takes control of Milan.

1453

Constantinople falls to the Ottoman Turks. This causes an exodus of Greek scholars, writers, and teachers to Italy.

1454

Johannes Gutenberg, credited with inventing the movable-type printing press, produces a copy of the Bible.

1464

Lorenzo de Medici becomes duke of Florence. Called Lorenzo the Magnificent by the people of the city because of his magnanimous personality, he leads the area to its highest point during the Renaissance.

1471

Sixtus IV becomes pope.

1484

Sandro Botticelli (1444–1510) paints *Birth of Venus* for the Medici in Florence.

1492

Rodrigo Borgia becomes Pope Alexander VI, considered the most corrupt of the Renaissance popes.

1494

The Medici are removed from Florence. Girolamo Savonarola, a traveling priest, speaks out against the materialism of the Medici. He is successful in removing them from power but is burned as a heretic in 1495.

1503

Julius II becomes pope. Leonardo da Vinci (1452–1519) paints the *Mona Lisa*.

1508–1512

Michelangelo Buonarroti (1475–1564) paints the ceiling of the Sistine Chapel.

1513

Pope Leo X, the son of Lorenzo de Medici, comes to power. Niccolò Machiavelli publishes *The Prince*.

1517

Martin Luther posts Ninety-five Theses on the door of the church in Wittenberg, Germany, starting the Protestant Reformation.

1519

Leonardo da Vinci dies.

1523

Pope Clement VII is appointed.

May 6, 1527

During the sack of Rome, Clement VII refuses to pay a ransom to the imperial army. The army then attacks the city and takes control. This is often called the end of the Renaissance.

For Further Research

Books

James Barter, *History Makers: Artists of the Renaissance*. San Diego: Lucent Books, 1999.

———, *A Travel Guide to Renaissance Florence*. San Diego: Lucent Books, 2002.

———, *The Working Life: A Renaissance Painter's Studio*. San Diego: Lucent Books, 2002.

Gene Brucker, *Renaissance Florence*. Berkeley and Los Angeles: University of California Press, 1983.

———, *Two Memoirs of Renaissance Florence: The Diaries of Buonaccorso Pitti and Gregorio Dati*. New York: Harper & Row, 1967.

Jacob Burckhardt, *The Civilization of the Renaissance in Italy*. New York: Penguin, 1990.

Peter Burke, *The Italian Renaissance: Culture and Society in Italy*. Princeton, NJ: Princeton University Press, 1999.

———, *Varieties of Cultural History*. Ithaca, NY: Cornell University Press, 1997.

E.R. Chamberlin, *Everyday Life in Renaissance Times*. New York: Putnam, 1965.

Giovanni Ciappelli, *Art, Memory, and Family in Renaissance Florence*. Cambridge, England: Cambridge University Press, 2000.

Elizabeth S. Cohen and Thomas V. Cohen, *Daily Life in Renaissance Italy*. Westport, CT: Greenwood, 2001.

Bruce Cole, *Italian Art, 1250–1550: The Relation of Renaissance Art to Life and Society*. New York: Harper & Row, 1987.

———, *The Renaissance Artist at Work*. London: John Murray, 1983.

James A. Corrick, *The Renaissance*. San Diego: Lucent Books, 1998.

Claire Dorey, *History of Italian Art*. Cambridge, England: Polity, 1994.

Editors of Time-Life, *What Life Was Like at the Rebirth of Genius: Renaissance Italy, A.D. 1400–1550*. Alexandria, VA: Time-Life Books, 1999.

Paul F. Grendler, *The Renaissance: An Encyclopedia for Students*. New York: Charles Scribner's Sons, 2004.

———, ed., *Encyclopedia of the Renaissance*. New York: Scribner's, 1999.

J.R. Hale, ed., *A Concise Encyclopaedia of the Italian Renaissance*. New York: Oxford University Press, 1981.

Frederick Hartt, *History of Italian Renaissance Art: Painting, Sculpture, Architecture*. New York: II.N. Abrams, 1994.

Jeff Hay, ed., *World History by Era, Vol. 4: The Renaissance*. San Diego: Greenhaven, 2001.

George Holmes, *Renaissance*. New York: St. Martin's, 1996.

Paul Oskar Kristeller, *Renaissance Thought and the Arts: Collected Essays*. Princeton, NJ: Princeton University Press, 1990.

Jean Lucas-Dubreton, *Daily Life in Florence in the Time of the Medici*. New York: Macmillan, 1961.

David Mateer, ed., *Courts, Patrons, and Poets: The Renaissance in Europe*. New Haven, CT: Yale University Press, 2000.

Patricia D. Netzley, *The Way People Live: Life During the Renaissance*. San Diego: Lucent Books, 1997.

Raymond Obstfeld and Loretta Obstfeld, eds., *History Firsthand: The Renaissance*. San Diego: Greenhaven, 2002.

J.H. Plumb, *Horizon Book of the Renaissance*. New York: American Heritage, 1961.

Stephen P. Thompson, ed., *Literary Movements and Genres: Renaissance Literature*. San Diego: Greenhaven, 2001.

———, *Turning Points in World History: The Renaissance*. San Diego: Greenhaven, 2000.

Paola Tinagli, *Women in Italian Renaissance Art: Gender, Representation, Identity*. Manchester, England: Manchester University Press, 1997.

Timothy Verdon and John Henderson, *Christianity and the Renaissance: Image and Religious Imagination in the Quattrocento*. Syracuse, NY: Syracuse University Press, 1990.

Evelyn S. Welch, *Art and Society in Italy, 1350–1500*. Oxford, England: Oxford University Press, 1997.

Periodicals

Moshe Arkin, "'One of the Marys . . .': An Interdisciplinary Analysis of Michelangelo's Florentine Pieta," *Art Bulletin*, September 1997.

Antonia Bostrom, Alan P. Darr, and Larry J. Feinberg, "The Medici, Michelangelo, and the Art of Florence," *USA Today Magazine*, January 2003.

Paula Findlen, "Possessing the Past: The Material World of the Italian Renaissance," *American Historical Review*, February 1998.

Paul Grendler, "Form and Function in Italian Renaissance Popular Books," *Renaissance Quarterly*, Autumn 1993.

Craig Harbison, "Meaning in Venetian Renaissance Art: The Issues of Artistic Ingenuity and Oral Tradition," *Art History*, March 1992.

Hilarie M. Sheets, "Renaissance Women," *Art News*, January 2003.

Deanna Shemek, "Circular Definitions: Configuring Gender in Italian Renaissance Festival," *Renaissance Quarterly*, Spring 1995.

Joanna Woods-Marsden, "Toward a History of Art Patronage in the Renaissance: The Case of Pietro Aretino," *Journal of Medieval and Renaissance Studies*, Spring 1994.

Web Sites

Architecture in Renaissance Italy, www.metmuseum.org/toah/hd/itar/hd_itar.htm. From the Metropolitan Museum of Art in New York, this site gives an overview of Brunelleschi, Alberti, and Palladio, the three greatest Renaissance architects. There are also links to photos of their works and to other sites that deal with architecture during the Renaissance.

The Civilization of the Renaissance in Italy, www.boisestate.edu/courses/hy309/docs/burckhardt/burckhardt.html. This site provides an online version of the book by Jacob Burckhardt, which is considered one of the greatest works on the Renaissance.

A Guide to Medieval and Renaissance Instruments, www.s-hamilton.k12.ia.us/antiqua/instrumt.html. This site is a guide to various Renaissance musical instruments, with descriptions, images, and audio samples of each.

Internet Medieval Sourcebook, www.fordham.edu/halsall/sbook1 x.html. This site contains one of the more complete listings of primary Renaissance documents available on the Web.

Italian Renaissance Architecture, http://rubens.anu.edu.au/htdo cs/surveys/italren/renarch. A collection of photographs of famous Renaissance architecture, grouped by the architect.

Medici Archive Project, www.medici.org. This nonprofit organization has made available the archive of the Medici grand dukes of Tuscany. This record of the greatest family of the Renaissance offers an insight into their rule.

Renaissance, www.learner.org/exhibits/renaissance. Produced by Annenberg/CPB, this site is set up as a resource for teachers. It contains a wealth of knowledge and a variety of articles.

Renaissance Links on the WWW, www.twingroves.district96.k12. il.us/renaissance/GeneralFiles/RenLinksGen.html. A collection of Web sites that cover art, architecture, daily life, law, medicine, and more. The sites' links vary in quality, but are generally good.

Renaissance Web Links, www.historyteacher.net/APEuroCourse/ WebLinks/WebLinks-Renaissance.html. An extensive list of Web resources, including both primary and secondary sources.

16th-Century Art Italy: The High Renaissance and Mannerism, http://witcombe.sbc.edu/ARTH16thcentury.html#Italy16. An extensive listing of artists and their works compiled by Christopher L.C.E. Witcombe, professor of art history at Sweet Briar College, Virginia.

Index

Gloucester Library
P.O. Box 2380
Gloucester, VA 23061